The BOAT KID

MEMOIRS...

and Life's Lessons Learned

To Jill
From Ron

RON F. KINSELLA

The BOAT KID
– Memoirs and Life's Lessons Learned
Copyright © 2014 by Ron F. Kinsella. All rights reserved.

rfkinsella83@gmail.com

www.TheBoatKidbooks.com

ISBN: 978-0-9907521-1-0 (pbk.)

PCN: 2014920216

Category: History / American History / Biography / Creative Non-Fiction

Cover Photo by: Austin Kinsella

Book Cover Design and Digital Formatting / Layout by:
Eli Blyden | www.CrunchTimeGraphics.com

Printed in the United States of America

For Mom, always so generous

CONTENTS

FOREWORD

I had thought that my life story as a kid could all fit onto one yellow sticky note. I was wrong. It became a *book* of sticky notes, and then finally what you are now seeing. Unlike so many other stories you may read, all of these are true, with most parts being exactly as I remember them, and some with details my sister and mother provided.

Granted, writing a book about real-life situations from a kid's perspective may not seem like a wise thing to do, at least from a sales standpoint. After all, we live in an age when there seems to be a strong desire to disconnect from reality. Young readers seem to be highly interested in fantasy or other fiction-type novels. There are so many of them on the market. This only fueled my desire to put these simple and true stories on paper, and have the young (and the young at heart) be my primary aim. Besides, making a sale is not all there is to life anyway. I thank you for looking, whether you decide to make this book your own or not.

Really, all the events in these stories could have happened to nearly anyone. In fact, everyone will have their own special experiences. Each experience gained often comes with its associated lesson learned. Some of which we will not fully understand the meaning of and its impact on our lives and our thinking until maybe much later in life. I have included at the end of most of the stories what could be called "lessons learned." This part, printed in italics, is what I think was gained from the experience. Maybe you can relate to some of them. But more importantly I hope you can benefit from them in some way.

It is also my hope that you have at least half the enjoyment reading these stories as I did in writing them.

–From my family to yours

CHAPTER ONE:

Silver Overboard!

I know, just the mention of silver in the chapter's title has stirred up in your mind thoughts of a story of pirate lore and treasure chests, with silver pieces of eight tossed overboard, right? Well, that is good, because this really *is* a story of lost silver. Let me explain.

It was a sunny, beautiful morning at the island just west of Carter Cay in the northern Bahamas. We were vacationing on our boat, anchored in what my dad called "Hurricane Hole," although the local name for it is "The Hogsty." This was a deep, clear natural lagoon located at the island's center. We were feeling great after a good night's sleep, and we were all just having a great morning together. We had our breakfast, which consisted of pretty much the usual: lobster and eggs.

My younger brother Joe and I happily took up our assignment of washing the silver we were carrying with us. This new boat we had did not have a sink installed yet, so the "final rinse" stage of silver-washing was done by leaning over the side of the boat, letting water fill the washtub, and rinsing the silver. Yes, as young kids, leaning over the side without falling in was a feat in itself. This was a two-person project, to be handled quickly before you passed out from being practically upside down. And yet it was to be done thoroughly as you did not care to repeat this step. Nothing to it, right? Just an ordinary chore.

This morning, though, *it happened.* To this day, we are not certain as to which one of us dropped our end of the tub, but it happened. It was like the worst scene straight out of a horror movie. All the silver tumbled out of the washtub.

My brother and I watched, silent, as all the precious metal flipped, spun, and twirled its way down, down through the crystal clear water, all the way until each piece finally came to rest peacefully on the bottom of the lagoon. Neither one of us spoke a word. *What do we do?* each of us was thinking as we gazed at all of it down there, glistening in the morning sun.

A certain, all-too-familiar sick feeling in the stomach began to set in. And that weakness in your muscles that begins to sap your energy. Yes, it was a kid's nightmare. Fear gripped us both!

What's the problem? you say. Yes, what *is* the problem? And you rightfully ask, as my brother and I were quite used to free diving, up to twenty or twenty-five feet deep. We could often do this for up to a minute or longer at a time. Free diving, as it is called, is like scuba diving, only without air tanks. This was performed daily by us while out in the Bahamas or the Florida Keys. This morning, however, was going to be different, far different. You see, my brother and I had spent the previous evening and night in this very lagoon catching sharks, big ones. The kind you don't haul aboard. Instead, you have to just cut the line. In

fact, we kids decided to give the place its proper name: Shark Hole. In our minds at least, this place seemed to just crawl with them. Now you understand. There would be no free diving here, no sir.

So what do we do? What do we say? Do we deny it? Fortunately, we were not that short on common sense, but I must say, the thought did cross my mind. I looked around and took stock of the situation. Our sister, Kathie, was curled up in the cabin, reading a book. My mother, Marilyn, was using her "dog rag" to clean up the table and cooking area. Dad was whistling some tune as he rearranged one of his parts boxes. I looked back out at the day. It had changed. It had lost its beauty, and in fact, seemed very gloomy. Still, neither of us spoke, but we both knew what the other felt. Doom.

I sat down on the engine cover and thought of how I'd rather be sitting down in a dentist chair for a nice tooth pull. Maybe even a root canal. But you get the picture. This was just plain bad. Then, out of crazy fear or some unexplainable emotion, I just blurted it out: "We dropped the silver overboard!" I must have had the impulse thought that maybe if I just said it, the problem would kind of, well, go away. Or something. It didn't.

"Well, go and get it!" my dad calmly replied, and he resumed his whistling. We just sat there. *Doesn't he understand?* I asked myself. Of course he understood. What he understood was that this little dive should be no problem at all for us. There was really nothing to it. I began to ponder the outcome. *Are sharks vengeful? And*

do sharks think logically? I had wondered about this. Are they expecting us to serve them a human breakfast? But one fact I was certain of was this: that we did not have all day to think about this, as we were on our way down to the Abaco Islands, and as soon as the wiping and organizing was complete, the order to "up anchor" would be given, and our silver had better be on board. I drew on every drop of courage.

"Put your stuff on; we're going over!" I said in a commanding way to my little brother. So over the side we went, armed to the hilt with everything we could hold or strap on. We surely must have looked like something out of a James Bond movie. I, for one, was not going down without a fight.

It seemed to take an eternity to get to the bottom, before Joe could even begin to sack up all the precious, renegade silver. Upon reaching bottom, I guarded us both, scanning high, low, all around, and then high and low again. My mind was racing, my eyes frantically straining and searching out every distant shape, whether real or imagined, trying to detect whether or not the shape of a shark is beginning to materialize. *Is that a shark?* But I could not spend more than a second or two to make that determination, as I would need to begin scanning a new area. Two more eternities passed. *Why isn't he done yet?* I then recognized his hands pushing away from the bottom, to get himself upright instead of upside down. His quick nod told me he was finally done.

NASA would have been proud, as we must have looked like rockets blasting off, up to the surface with our silvery prize in tow. We scrambled up and into the boat. Sitting there at the stern, we pulled off our masks and took a big breath.

I was grinning from ear to ear, as my little brother was also, and we just sat there huffing and puffing, taking in the moment. We were alive! Settling down after a few minutes, I looked around. Kathie was still reading. Mom was finishing her wiping down everything with the dog rag. Dad was putting away his parts box. But something had seemed to change again. I then realized that it really was an incredibly *beautiful* day. *Life's good, real good*, I thought to myself.

But there's one more thing.

You see, this story is not about silver coins or silver treasure bars at all. Yes, silver, but of a somewhat lesser value. To be specific, it was our boat's *silverware*. That's right, the kind you eat with.

I began to ponder again. Are sharks really logical-minded, or not? As they had certainly seen all that silverware dropped overboard, surely they'd be expecting that breakfast would logically be served next. But none had showed up. Maybe they weren't the kind of thinkers that I thought they were. I would have to let it go for now, and resume my reasoning on it at a later time.

"I think we'll come up with another way to rinse," I said to Joe. "Yes, that's it."

There probably weren't any sharks even near us, and Dad and Mom always kept a watchful eye. Still, I had a newfound respect for my little brother after that. He was put to the test by me and followed my lead, fully trusting in me to protect him. I guess it was really a lesson on trust and respect for the both of us.

Second, the truth is, sometimes we can fret and worry ourselves sick over something until we're practically paralyzed with fear. Or, instead, we can "just dive in," so to speak, and get the job done.

Maybe it's not something fearful that holds us back, but something different. Maybe it's our own laziness, a lack of motivation that at times keeps us from getting things accomplished. We can waste precious time, make excuses, and frustrate others to no end. So next time, why not just go ahead and make things happen? Just dive in and do it!

. . .

I have included after some of the stories what you could call "sub-stories," to let you know about life on the boat.

"The Box":

Space was something we just didn't have a lot of. We kids had to pick and choose carefully what we brought, as it couldn't be much. We would sort through our stuff and make decisions on what toy or games we would bring. For Joe, which toy to bring; for Kathie, it was which books to bring. And, of course, just as important to her, what clothes to bring, just in case we went to Freeport, Hope Town, or Marsh Harbor. For my mom, it was our boat's supplies, and the dog rag, which you'll read about later.

Last, there was Dad's collection. Would he bring games, books, and nice clothes? Hardly. For him it was "The Box." What was in The Box, you ask? Well, if you must know, then I will have to give you the story behind my father. He can fix nearly anything. If he couldn't fix it, he would build a new one that was even better than what ever had broke, of course. And he believed in being prepared. For just about anything that could (and usually would) happen. I'm sure you already see where this is going. Yes, The Box was full of anything and everything useful. Two of every tool on the market, plus a spare. (Or so it seemed). Hose clamps, tape, putty, fuses, hoses, solder, torches, fiberglass repair, complete with roving cloth. Glue, gloves, wood parts, screws, bolts, propellers, cotter pins, string, brass fittings, snaps, nails. Starters, alternators, water pumps, and thermostats. We were like a floating, mobile "parts house." About the only thing we did not bring was our arc welder. The boat didn't produce the right kind of electricity to run it.

Now, mind you, I can only remember a time or two when our family actually needed any of this, for some minor repair or adjustments. But for the other boats traveling with us, we were a lifeline. "Ron, what in the world do you bring all that junk with you for?" would be some of the joking, sarcastic comments. Dad wouldn't say much to that. Somewhere into the trip, the requests would begin. "Would you happen to have an extra hose clamp or two, with some black tape, Ron? I've got a hose that's going bad." The next request would be something like: "That exhaust hose finally blew out, could I borrow a foot or so of the hose you brought?"

Dad was not about to let a blown hose spoil our trip, something he worked all year for.

He rarely would be found repairing something on our boat, but more often on someone else's and at times, a boat of someone who we didn't even know, but needed our help. It was at these times that us kids were told to "go back to our boat to get me a such-and-such out of The Box" on our boat. This was always an adventure. To Dad, a seemingly simple task of retrieving a gizmo or widget from our boat would turn into a disaster! Often he would first send one of us, then the second, and even the third of us kids back to help retrieve whatever it was he needed. I'm sure we made our fellow boaters think they'd seen something right out of a Three Stooges episode.

You see, The Box in the boat was actually a series of boxes, and boxes within boxes. Some of these boxes would not even be discovered until unloading the boat after a trip. The system was supposed to be actually quite simple, and I'm sure that for him, it was. Hose clamps go in cookie tin boxes. Impellers go in shoe boxes. Electrical parts go in cigar boxes, and so on. See the logic? It's OK—neither did we kids. But to a dad, it makes perfect sense, of course.

. . .

The Box (or, really, "Boxes") taught me the value of being organized, something I still need to work on. Especially on the more important things. His lists of stuff to bring are part of my archives, and I have learned to use lists now, helping me to think of and bring what I need, or may need.

Use lists to keep in mind your short-term and long-term goals. You could keep a running list of things that you always have to get done, and another, short list of the ones you plan to tackle for that week, or even that day. You'll get a lot more accomplished.

The other thing it taught me was to plan ahead. You may not always be able to guess what's going to be needed, but you can at least try. Don't travel "by the seat of your pants," as some say. You may have to use those pants to plug a hole. And then, what are you going to wear? Some people even say: "If it can go wrong, eventually it will go wrong." There seems to be some truth in that. So do what you can to be prepared. Whether it's just for your daily life, or for a three-week trip, it does pay to be organized and think ahead.

And then, there's the dilemma of what food to bring. But you'll have to read chapter two first, for that answer.

. . .

CHAPTER TWO:

Eye of the Shark

Some things in life are just inevitable, meaning they are just bound to happen, whether that be sooner or later. Some of those "things" I could easily do without. For example, if you come to spend enough time in the salty seas, you *will* run across a shark or two. Or, he will run across you, depending on whose point of view we're talking about here. Unfortunately, a shark's appearance with you is not like clockwork. But what you *can* count on, loosely, is this rule of thumb: when you're in the boat, and want to see a shark, you won't. When you're in the water and prefer *not* to see one is when it happens. Their appearance is very spontaneous, as if just "dropping in" on the party to check things out. It just happens, and it always takes you by surprise. I believe the shark gets some kind of satisfaction out of this. Probably the more times it happens, the easier it is for you when it happens.

Still, I don't care how many of those shark shows you watch on TV that remind you that sharks are our friends and "we just have to respect them." That all sounds real nice until you're in the water together with one. The shark no longer looks like the one on TV. You forget all those shows, and in your mind the built-in "fear-o-meter" gauge that we all have suddenly appears, with its pointer somewhere near the "panic" zone.

We had already had one incident at Barracouta Rocks where Dad, my little brother, Joe and I were free diving, and coming around an edge of this tiny volcanic island, all at once we spotted just the tail of a huge shark. He had his head and midsection in a round, ledged hole in the bottom. Again, just his very large tail was sticking out of the hole. He was hunting fish, but he must have sensed our presence, as we noticed him backing out of the hole. As we tried to quickly exit the area and retreat back around the corner, he fully emerged from the hole and began heading toward us at top speed. We were swimming as fast as we ever had, headed for the surface and the sharp, jagged ledge of the island. I took a fraction of a second for one last look as I approached the safety of the rocky top ledge. He was a hammerhead shark, probably about ten or eleven feet long. There was no time to do anything other than blast straight out of the water and up onto the razor-sharp outcropping of the rocks. Mom and my sister said it looked like three seals rocketing out of the water and up onto the ledge. Cut and bruised, we waited a long time to make our sprint through the water back to the boat. I felt a fear that I had not experienced before. Being a hammerhead shark, I never saw his eyes, as he was headed straight for us. Not seeing his eyes was actually a good thing.

But that is not all I have to say about sharks. Something else was to happen next year that would teach me a good lesson.

So here it is, the next summer, in the Florida Keys, with our family snorkeling and diving over a nice flat bottom with reef here and there, and coral heads that seemed to go on and on. It's one of the times in which we would not anchor, but simply drift—the boat, and all of us together in the water. Dad would have a floating rope out drifting also, and sometimes a small plastic boat, about the size of a bathtub. We kids could grab hold of the rope or get into the little boat if we were tired. The current would continually glide us over the reef, providing new scenery and fresh discoveries for us kids. It is a whole different world down there, with flora and fauna that are actually sea creatures that cannot be easily described. It is a world that is better if just observed and not touched. It's as if many of the corals and living things have an unseen, prickly covering, seemingly almost finer than frog's hair.

And the world down there is not a silent one, oh no. It is very noisy. A healthy reef can be almost deafening. Every large or tiny creature doing its job, of opening, waving, cleaning, closing, eating, and doing whatever else it is supposed to do. Each making its own particular sound: clapping, snapping, and popping. Millions upon millions of them. The orchestra all comes together to make one solid crescendo of percussion that even the most talented of conductors would be proud to preside over. As if in time with the orchestra, the sun's rays sparkle downward through the water, and dance on the seafloor. I wish you could actually hear and see it, because as I said before, the whole scenario cannot even really be described.

You may now be able to understand something, that this is how I could completely lose myself in this beautifully different undersea world. I'd hold my breath for a minute or two while swimming speedily along the bottom of the seabed's reef, through the forest-like landscape with sandy paths formed along the bottom by coral heads and sea fans, passing by all kinds of fish. I would pretend to be one of them, with only my need to rise for air reminding me that I was not. At each surfacing, I could take note of the direction of the boat and my family in the water with it, and make my course correction to try and keep up with them, as the current would carry us all along.

A Brush with the Eye

On this one such occasion, as I became somewhat distanced from the boat, *it happened.*

Looking around as I was heading to the surface, a big shark cruised right past me, and for a moment, we were eye-to-eye. The sight of him nearly stopped my heart, right there on the spot. That flushed, red-faced feeling you get, and then that cold feeling swept over me. The alarm of the fear-o-meter was blasting away in my head. I watched him cruise past me, and he faded away, behind me. But I knew what he was doing. He was sizing me up. I used the opportunity to get some air. *That's good, you didn't panic, he's gone now*, I thought. I headed back down, to the bottom, making good speed toward where I saw our boat last. My brush with a shark that close left me feeling uneasy, insecure. Then, out of nowhere, there he was *again*! About twenty-five feet away this time, and coming from my front again. *How did he do that? He was* behind *me!* As I swung my head around from the surprise, there he was again. But wait. It was all clear now. There were *two* sharks, not one. *Just don't panic, please, don't panic,* I begged myself. The other shark came cruising up beside me, not ten feet away. Again, our eyes met. I was certain that he could see the fear in mine.

Now, as you probably already know, some stories just aren't pretty, and do not always end well. Maybe right about now you're wondering—is this going to be a happy ending? Will I survive this one? If you're maybe even just a bit squeamish, you might want to quit this chapter right now. Nonetheless, I will leave it up to you whether you wish to continue or not. Of course, if you stop now, the question will forever remain in your mind, though—will it get better, or will it get worse? This is your last chance to turn back.

It Gets Far Worse

OK, *that* just gave it away. So you might as well keep reading. But first, let me indulge you a little about my previous findings down here in the watery world. Let's start over.

The Eyes Have It

I had already seen and took note of many a sea creature's eyes. Like the wavy string of pretty blue eyes of the scallop, as he sees you and tries desperately to flit away from you, opening and closing his shell halves as rapidly as he can, propelling him somewhat precariously. Or the blueberry-on-a-stalk eyes of the lobster, as he waves his two antennas at you as if to say, "stay away!" Then, there's the mysterious eye-sticking-out-of-the-sand of the flounder, lying on the bottom, his body covered with sand, wondering if you've discovered him. The funny, almost surprised look of the puffer fish's eyes. And the glaring looks from the Goliath grouper's eyes, as he inspects you, while you inspect him.

Yes, *the eyes*. And the eyes out here are all so very different from ours. But there is one sea creature's eyes that I will never forget. They were the eyes of a small lost seal, battered and bleeding, that my sister and I had come across while exploring a jagged lava-rock section of what I think was either Spanish Cay or Powell Cay. How he got there I will never know, as we had never seen a seal around the Bahamas anywhere before. Kathie and I approached him, and he allowed us to get right up close to him.

They say that the eyes are the windows to the heart and mind, and I firmly believe that. They seem to embody who we are. When we talk to someone, we look at their eyes. Not their ears, not their nose. The eyes are it. They are truly special. And as I peered into this seal's eyes, and he into mine, I felt something very, very familiar. Yes, I had seen this look before. But where? It hit me. Yes, it was the look of our family dog's eyes, Happy. Old and wise for a dog, we spent much time together. We could gaze into each other's eyes for long periods of time, with a certain kind of understanding that needs no words.

Now, as I looked at this seal I was taken aback, as he had the eyes you do not expect to see out here in this watery world, in the middle of nowhere. They were so different from the eyes of the other creatures he shared the ocean with. He seemed to know we meant no harm. He had an anxious, almost questioning look in his eyes. I imagine he was asking, "Have you seen my family?" "Do you know which way is home?" It was really hard to leave the owner of those eyes, as I had no answers for him. After telling Dad and Mom about him, they assured us that there was not much we could do for a wild seal out here. I had to convince myself that despite everything so familiar about him, he was not another lost dog that we could just simply take home. I hope he recovered.

OK, where *were* we? Oh yes, the sharks. Well, my point in saying all that was that the shark's eyes had no emotion, but instead were ever so cold, calculating. Just the kind of eyes you would expect if you came face-to-face with a relentless eating machine. That look of his, combined with the closeness of him next to me, had the fear-o-meter in my head glowing red, with the needle way past the "panic" zone on the dial.

I thought of how that food-chain poster on the wall of Mr. Steadham's 6B classroom was horribly inaccurate! I did not feel that I was anywhere near the top of the chain at that moment. So what do I do about my predicament? I had seen every *Sea Hunt* episode on TV and, for a brief second, thought, *What would Lloyd Bridges do?* I really didn't know, so I just thought: *Don't head for the surface; you'll panic and thrash like a wounded fish.* I headed lower to get away from them, and sped at top speed through the street-like paths on the bottom. However, it wouldn't be long before I would need air, and would have to surface again. *This seems to be working,* I thought. *Stay low, don't be at their level.* I would head up, get some air, check on the boat's location, and head back for the bottom, posthaste.

Fortunately for me, I thought, sharks must not be very good at geometry. Yes, his eyes were cold and calculating, as I had mentioned. But they must not have been calculating too well, as they were obviously still working on sizing me up. I was just a kid, and I could clearly see that they were twice or three times my size. And I had not even taken geometry! I then got worried he would give up on the complex math, and decide to go straight to some simple division: into how many bites should he divide me up?

I knew it was time to act, and fast, so I decided to make my move. I began my sharp angle for the surface, at top speed. Even though I was like a torpedo trying to go as fast as possible, still, I could not resist the urge to quickly look all around. Doing so, my heart sank. I counted: one, two, *three* sharks now! I was encircled! It was like the fear-o-meter now exploded, sending shards of superheated shrapnel ricocheting painfully inside my head, and it became hard to even think. I begged myself again: *You've got to* keep calm *just a few more seconds, please. When you hit the surface, don't thrash!*

My head broke the surface, and I rose halfway out of the water from the tremendous speed I still had. I had guessed right! The boat was in my view, and not far off! My timing couldn't have been more perfect. Everyone was in the boat, and Mom was searching in my direction at that very instant. *Now's your chance*, I thought: *take it!*

"Sharks!" I yelled out as loud as I could. Mom began pointing to me, alerting Dad to my plight and position. As Dad quickly started the boat and headed toward me, the circling sharks began to back off, perhaps alerted to the sound of the propeller. I quickly jumped on the back of the boat as it passed by, and sat on the back ladder for a minute.

I was grateful I had pulled off what I thought was an amazing escape for a kid.

The Resolution

"Got into a little trouble out there, huh?" Dad said.

"Yeah," I replied, trying to sound brave about it now, after screaming like a stuck pig earlier.

"Stay closer to the boat next time, so you can stay in sight," he said.

"Yeah," I responded. But in my mind I had already resolved that this was not going to happen again. "You know, those sharks are probably still down there," he added as a little reminder. This was because I was so relieved to be sitting there, just thinking, and I had forgotten that my legs were still hanging down in the water! In a split second,

I went from sitting to standing, getting every inch of me out of the water.

I made two more resolutions. With a red marker, I would correct the food-chain chart in 6B, for the benefit of the next students after me.

The second was more personal. I may be constantly reminded that I forget a lot of things. I may not remember much that happens on a day-to-day basis. But I had seen something down there that I'd *never* forget: My close encounter, with *the eye of the shark!*

. . .

In reality, the sharks probably were just curious, and already well fed. Something I realized that same day was that my pretending could get me into trouble, and fast. Always keep an eye on your surroundings, and be aware of what's going on. Stay close to safety—in my case, it was the boat. Yes, my family had noticed that I was too far away and not keeping up, so they were already coming for me. But don't count on someone always being able to rescue you. Do your best to be safe, so that you and whoever's with you can enjoy even more whatever it is you are doing.

. . .

Boat food:

There is a term some use for this kind of vacation boating. They call it bare-boating. For us it was just boating. But "bare-boating" really is a good term. It's not that your boat is completely bare, of course: there is a cabin, a top, motors, some food, etc. It's just that you don't seem to have much of anything else. Only the basics, and for two good reasons: room, and weight. You don't have room in the boat for more, and it can't carry all the weight of anything "extra" anyway. Sure, you'd love to bring two or three weeks' worth of water, but you just can't. And then there's food. Things like Twinkies or Cocoa Puffs? Hah! They're totally useless as you don't have milk with you anyway. Sodas? Forget that. Way too heavy, and there's no room in the cooler to keep them cool. And you wouldn't dare chip at your ice block to put some ice chips in your glass. You may not find ice for another week. Ever had *hot* soda? I think you get the point. Dessert would be some chopped-up pieces of a coconut you had found, with the possibility of a pinch of sugar on it if you could get your hands on some. Coconut is not actually that sweet on its own.

On these trips you pretty much eat whatever you find or catch and cook that day, which was almost the same every day. The only game-changers were what we would bring to vary things a little. This was accomplished by bringing some of the factory-fresh foods like canned ham, or better yet, SPAM, which is meat you don't need a knife for. There were cans of pork and beans, yams, corn, and, of course, those little canned sausages. Cases of them. (Do the Austrians really eat them?) How those tasty little pieces of whatnot became a favorite among boat people is, I suppose, a mystery that I must research some day. I too had succumbed to the irresistible flavor of this little delicacy. The specific procedure to eating them is not advertised; it must be learned. As a rule, you do not read the ingredients. The rule applies to many foods, but out here, you just don't have time. You are fishing. And you are really hungry. The ingredients must be imagined to be whatever sounds right.

At the factory, the sausages are bundled, about six together, and a metal can is shrink-wrapped around them to prevent you from removing them easily. Any attempt at removing the first one by use of needle-nose pliers or the like only turns the hapless sausage into an unappetizing, useless mush. Use your bait-cutting, fishy fingers for the job.

So, you have that first one removed, do you? Toss it over the side as you probably resorted to the needle-nose pliers I told you not to use. You could use some chum in the water anyway, as the fish have not been biting. Then, enjoy one of life's simple pleasures—the Vienna sausage!

The Boat Kid

.

28

CHAPTER THREE:

"What in the World Was *That?*"

D o you ever have a craving for something at times? Maybe for your favorite candy bar? For me, it's a good flan, or my mom's bread-and-raisin custard pudding. Or maybe it's her key lime pie. Could be a vanilla malt, or a bacon, lettuce, and tomato sandwich, better known as the "BLT." I guess I have many. We'll pick up this story after I visit the kitchen.

OK, I'm back. Yes, those cravings for a treat, something special we enjoy. For some kids, it's soda. Cola, root beer, orange or grape soda, whichever. But not me. We just didn't get to have a lot of that, even when at home. Mom just didn't buy it, unless they were having others over. The kids in class would even talk about secretly bringing it for lunch at school, daring each other about it. You see, soda at my little school was not allowed. The choice was milk, chocolate milk, or orange juice. Seeing the issue, I decided one day that I would bravely bring Coca-Cola to class, and present it to myself for all to see during lunch, except for the teacher, of course.

Some plans are just doomed from the start. About ten a.m., from the back of the classroom came a loud *pow!* with the sound of shattering glass, followed by a fizzing noise. Everyone's head then turned to the back of the room, and some were quick to identify it. "It's coming from Ronnie's lunch box!" The entire 4B class and our teacher, Mrs. Beulah Young, watched in horror as the soda's foam came oozing from my red plaid lunch box and began flowing down over all the lower shelves. My heart started going crazy, and the sweating started. I knew that I was finished. The glass thermos I had put the Coke in had exploded from the pressure as it warmed up. Yes, the laws of physics had won, *again*! So much for my well thought out plan. But there was a price to pay for such brazen behavior. That lump in my throat, the dry-mouth-and-shaky-hands feeling swept over me as I thought about what would happen to me next.

"Ronnie Kinsella! Is that *your* lunchbox?" It was Mrs. Young's stern reaction to the fiasco.

"Yes Ma'am, it is" came my feeble reply.

Sentence and justice on me was meted out quickly in front of the class with Mrs. Young's Ping-Pong paddle. That's right, a paddling. I both loved and respected Mrs. Young's being wise and strict, and had full confidence in every decision she made. Her discipline on me that day did not change how I felt about her. But something else did change. Yes, after that experience, soda was maybe now much farther down my list of favorite things.

However, this is not a story about the joys of school, so I'll get back on track. *Yes, why all this about soda,* you're wondering. Well, as I mentioned earlier, our trips usually had little or no luxury items, and soda was a luxury item. If the other families' kids had managed to get some cans of the stuff on board, they were few and gone quickly. And in the sparsely inhabited out-islands, there often is no grocery store or soda vending machine to pull up and put your money into. For some kids, the situation without their sodas was, well, in a word: *desperate.*

On this one particular trip, I would finally experience the real joys of soda. I don't know whether the kids on the other boats asked, or how it really got started. But just imagine the kids' surprise one day as we had pulled up to a village's gas dock with our boats, at an island that will go unmentioned, where the attendant said to some of the kids with us: "I know a man back in the village who has *sodas,* lots of them, for cheap." Well, the clamoring, begging and pleading from the kids began. Finally, the dads decided to go inland and seal the deal on this unheard-of bargain to be had, while the kids waited in agony.

A while later they returned with the liquid loot in tow. They had a whole case of it. Ten or so were loaded into our deep ice chest, to begin cooling them down for later. Having gotten our supplies and fuel, we started all engines and our boats all left the dock and began our next leg of the trip for the day. Interested in the new drinks, I took a few minutes to examine this sought-after treasure. Sure enough, it was soda, even a store brand I recognized. However, I didn't recognize the name of the flavor. It was cream-something, which I really don't remember. It's possible that my mind does not want to remember, because my sister and I decided first to try a can of it ourselves.

That was a big mistake. We popped a top. *Hmm. Sounds normal.* We took the first swig. Then, we blew it back out so hard we nearly passed out. "What in the world is this stuff? It's horrible!" we said. It had sort of a fizzy, salty-olive flavor that was just plain *bad.* What had gone wrong at the soda factory? Had a worker accidentally hung his coat on the olive-flavoring lever that day? On top of that, they must have gotten a patent on some type of syrupy formula that made the stuff extra sticky. You could hardly wash it out of your mouth.

It was then that the wheels of thought began to churn again. *Hmm.* "Are you thinking what I'm thinking?" asked Kathie.

"Yep," I replied. I was on board for this one. Maybe trying it out first was not a mistake after all. Needless to say, the plans were then laid for a little surprise for our friends in the other boats. Later in the day, reaching a good spot to spend the night at New Plymouth, Green Turtle Cay, the precious sodas were retrieved from the icebox by the other kids. Anxiously popping the tops, they all began to take that first cold, dreamy, wonderful slurp that you would expect. Kathie and I watched quietly. Then, *we got the results.* The gagging started. Followed by hiccups, snorts, and nose spurts. One by one, just seconds apart, every one of them began running to the side of the boat, the nasty stuff spraying from their mouths and noses. "Blech!" "Yuck!" "What is this stuff?" and "I feel sick" were heard. Enjoying the sight to the full, my sister said "I like to think of it as olive soda."

"Why didn't you tell us?" one of them asked.

"Because you wouldn't have believed us anyway. You would have said that we only wanted the sodas for ourselves," came Kathie's reply. How could we do this to them? Well, I must say that my sister did have a motive for this sly trick we played on them. People would say that she *was*, and even *looked* a lot like Charlie Brown's older sister, Lucy. You see, my sister is a testy thing who can invent intimidating words as required on the fly. She could keep the other kids at bay, and send even the older boys scurrying for cover with her sharp tongue and biting wit. Because of this, she had the inevitable fate to be forever the target of let's-get-even-with-her!-type schemes, for which she would gladly dish out more in return.

Earlier, when one of them threw a messy-looking plastic throw-up puddle next to her, it had started all over again. He had waited for just the right moment, when she turned the right shade of green from already being seasick, and then plopped it down in front of her, sending her running for the side of the boat, releasing the most recent meal. I knew she would be brewing up another scheme soon. The olive soda was just what we needed, and the stuff served its purpose well. Kathie and I were laughing and gloating over our victory as they were rinsing their mouths. Then, on one of their faces there was, a look. A smile, maybe more like a smirk. Then, another, with a glance. All of a sudden, *it happened.* There was no time to think. There was a mad rush for the soda cans, which were grabbed up, shaken, pointed at us, and we were now thrown into the middle of an all-out, no-holds-barred, shake-and-point soda-spray *party!* The foamy soda was shooting at us from all directions, like fireworks! We too grabbed up our cans and began returning fire! There was squealing and laughs as each team scored well with every glorious can. In a minute or so, it was all over. We were out of sodas. All of us were drenched in the stinky, sticky stuff. Yes, they had gotten us good, but it had been great! *Well done!*

Our only regret was that none of us thought that day to save a can of the stuff for the Ripley's Believe It or Not! museum. Whatever the deal was with the stuff, we may never know and I guess it really doesn't matter—just one of life's mysteries.

Still, someday I'm going to write that soda company, first to let them know how much fun that soda was, and of course to ask: "Really now, what in the world was that?"

. . .

About the only lesson I got out of what happened out there is this: to be wary when somebody has a "deal" that's just too good to be true. If it's that good, why hasn't anybody else bought it?

On second thought, I guess there really is one more thing learned from that experience: that you can have fun with even the simplest of things in life, even a can of soda.

. . .

Breakfast:

Breakfast on the boat was always interesting in its own way. Sometimes I would try to actually sleep in, as we kids call it, or sleep too long, as adults say. This was usually because of our watching for comets or star-gazing. OK, we were really visiting with the neighboring boat's kids until late in the night. Eventually we kids would make our beds, such as the one at the boat's dining table, which was basically a table that would lower to being level with the booth seats on each side, becoming a bed.

The awakening for us kids in the morning would be a harsh one. *Bang! Bang! Bang! Bang!* Yes, it was the all-too-familiar metal-on-metal sound of my dad banging on the pipes of our boat's gas stove. He said the pipes would get dirt in them and would not burn clean, and so all the annoying ruckus was to loosen the dirt and rust from the pipes. We kids weren't sure that this procedure was absolutely necessary. Really now, was *every* stove built with this obvious design flaw? *Why don't we hear that coming from other people's boats too?*—we would think to ourselves. Anyway, once awake, I was still not ready to get up. Because, you see, as I lay in my bed, perched just above my head was another old friend of a different kind. I like to think of it as Radio City. But I'll save that for chapter four.

CHAPTER FOUR:

Friends of Merritt

Ok, so you've noticed that my spelling is not that great. Is it "merit" or "Merritt"? You know what I mean, anyway, right? Or do you? Well, read on and find out.

It was another summer vacation on the boat, and our thirty-foot Jersey was docked in the marina of the hotel at West End, on Grand Bahama Island. It had been a really bad crossing of the Straits, from Florida to West End. It was the first time for us kids. We had never seen such mountainous waves as those before. So we were really happy to be spending the days exploring, fishing, snorkeling, and just being lazy in our inner tubes in the crystal clear water of the small islands around West End. Evenings and nights were then spent docked in the marina. The hotel had some great dock parties and dinners for the ones like us staying on their dock, which were a lot of fun, with locals and hotel staff providing entertainment and live music, Bahamian style. Still, even with all this, something began to feel amiss with me. As usual, no matter where I was, and however much fun we were having, something would change. I would begin to miss my friends back home. Yes, a really crazy feeling indeed, as I well knew that summer would be over all too soon and I would be back at school with them. Then I would begin wishing that we were back on the boat somewhere! Unexpectedly, though, things were about to change for me.

We'd had another great day out on the boat, with the usual fishing, snorkeling, and plunking around. While cruising back to our marina, we kids discovered some Pay Day candy bars we had bought back in Riviera Beach, and then stored away on the boat. We had walked to a drugstore there, just across the Blue Heron Bridge, back on the mainland side. The candy, it seemed, we had forgotten all about until now, and it was a fun surprise to find the forgotten loot. It didn't even matter that they were all melted, a chocolate gooey mess from the heat. They were so good. But today's surprise treats were not over. This day would prove to be different.

As we made our entry into the marina, I could see things had changed while we were gone. We had neighbors! A boat a little smaller than ours, docked in the slip right next to ours! But there was no time to gawk, as we were getting ready to dock. As usual, I took my station on the bow, ready to grab the mooring lines as Dad would have us get our bow ropes to the front pilings first, and then ease the boat back toward the seawall and secure the stern. This was not easy docking, as there were only pilings (wooden posts) for the bow. There was no dock at the *side* of the boat. Only at the stern. My mom and Kathie would handle the rear lines. My little brother, being only five years old, still had passenger status and had not yet been conscripted into crew service. His time would come. Still, we put him to work anyway, doing whatever Kathie and I asked him to do. Docking was an exact science to Dad, and, though he had a very unscientific crew to work with, we often could pull off docking maneuvers that could have made even Jack Sparrow shed a joyful tear.

Once docked and I was dismissed, I moved in for a closer look. Yes, she was a beauty. It was a T-Craft, the first I'd seen, about twenty-three feet long. They had evidently just arrived as they were still flying their yellow quarantine flag on the boat's antennae. The Bahamian government required that any visitors from other countries stay on their boat until they had been cleared by the emigrations authorities. The sharply dressed officers were standing on the dock just behind their boat.

Then, *it happened.*

Kneeling at the engine box, filling out her emigrations papers with pen in hand, was a girl about my age. *Yes!* I thought to myself. *Not exactly another young guy like me, but she'll do just fine!*

A yell from behind her in the boat broke my fixation on her. "Honey, you can't let her fill that out—this is *important* stuff!" a stern voice said. It was her father, saying this to the girl's mother. Alarmed, as he was talking about her, the girl quickly looked up, and our eyes met. I wanted to just disappear, but I couldn't. So I gave her one of those sympathetic looks, the kind your mom gives you when you used to run into the house with your skinned knees from falling off your bike. Overwhelmed with embarrassment from the scene, she quickly dropped her head into her arms, hiding her face. I made my exit, sparing her any further embarrassment. Getting back on our boat, I tried not to look any more, even though they were "berthed," or parked, right next to us.

My parents were always meeting new people, and made friends everywhere. Dad somehow always ended up attracting people who needed something fixed on their boat. His boat parts "box" was a big attraction, I guess. As it turned out, our new neighbors were just plain friendly, and didn't need anything fixed at all. They were coastal lovers like us, very tan from summers and weekends spent on the water. The girl's father, nicknamed "Lucky," was found to be really a good people-friendly dad, so it was not long before both our families got acquainted and were enjoying each other. There were five of them: Lucky, his wife, the girl, her college-aged sister, and a friend.

We spent the next few days taking the boats out, exploring the waters of this little corner of the Atlantic with them, visiting Indian Cay, Sandy Cay, and other spots, and enjoying each other's company. While snorkeling under the hot sun, in the clear, warm waters of Sandy Cay, with my new friend, I managed my first run-in with a spiny little creature called the sea urchin. It's the porcupine of the urchin family. Taking a break from snorkeling for a few minutes, I put my foot down on the bottom, and stepped right on the urchin. Doing this buried one of its long black, needlelike spines through my swim fin and deep into my heel, where it broke off.

"Let's swim over to my boat and I can get that out," she said. While we ate sandwiches she had made, I reclined

on her boat, and she assessed the damage to my foot. I gladly soaked up all the attention. I asked where she and her family were from. "Merritt Island," came her reply.

"I don't think I know where that is," I said.

"Where are you from?" she asked.

"Land O' Lakes," I said.

"I don't know where that is either, but I think my mom buys our butter from there," she said. She poked and prodded on my foot for quite some time. We talked about many things, but neither of us brought up age. Age *is* kind of an awkward thing to kids. It can be overly important. In this case, I was nine. Nine is important, because it's just short of ten. Ten is very significant as there is just something about that extra digit that makes you an adult in the eyes of the single-digit-aged kids. I suspected she was already there, but neither of us brought up this subject. Maybe because we both knew how it usually changes the dynamics of a friendship when you're a kid. As the younger one, you always wish it didn't factor into things.

"I can't get the spine out," she finally said with a sigh in her voice, as she dropped her hands and quit working on my foot.

"It's OK, maybe my mom can," I replied. Little did I know that it would be days before I could put any weight on my foot again, and months before it would be somewhat back to normal.

The day finally came for us to have to leave and head back to Florida. Both of our dads decided it would be best to leave together, as it's just safer that way. As we headed across the Straits, it was a rather calm, blue-sky type day, with only gentle, rolling swells, like small hills over open meadows. For most of the long journey back, I stayed seated at the rear of our boat, so she could see me and I could catch a glimpse of her every now and then. As we bounded over the deep blue Atlantic, the song "98.6" was playing over and over in my head.

Then, *it happened.* I noticed their boat began pulling away from ours. Reacting, I scurried up to the fly bridge, wounded foot and all. I yelled over the sound of the engines and spray, "Dad, there's something wrong! They're not staying with us!"

"It's OK, they're going home," he replied in his matter-of-fact way.

My mind racing, I thought, No, this is not "OK." *And just where is home? How will we find them again? I don't know their last name. I don't even know where Merritt Island is.*

Stuck in the mire of confusion and disappointment, I watched as their boat slowly drew farther and farther off to our starboard side, until becoming a tiny white spec on the horizon. Finally they faded out of sight.

My new friend had left as quickly as she came.

When we were finally back home, other things to be concerned with quickly took over. School would be starting again, and each time has its own newness, with its changes and summer stories to share with the same friends you had from before, and the possibilities of new friendships to be made.

And, of course, the question of: *who* we would meet *next* summer?

. . .

You, like me, have probably come to embrace these thoughts about friendships: to make a friend, be a friend. Friends come in all shapes, sizes, and colors. And that age is really not important among friends. None of that matters. Important is that you start making them early on in your life, and do not let opportunities to make friends pass you by. Yes, you will lose some of them to time and circumstance, but if you worry about this too much, you'll be too afraid to make a friend.

A word of caution, though —Just because someone demands your attention does not make them a friend. People you meet on social media may not be your friends. A friend should be someone you have come to know well, and trust. Choose the ones that help move you to do what is good, and want you to succeed. Choose them wisely.

Making a friend is like giving a gift to yourself. And who doesn't like getting gifts? So enrich your life with friends!

And, yes, I now know where Merritt Island is.

. . .

Radio City:

Actually, this "old friend" was our ship-to-shore radio. It was a huge radio and telephone combined, and it was really our only connection with the world. With it we got news. We could talk to the other boaters, anywhere. We could even call home. And, even better, we got the Bahamian radio stations' music! Dad would have it on in the mornings and evenings, playing the local's soft, gentle island music, so different from back home. It was the greatest, most relaxing thing to enjoy. Even the commercials were so different and interesting, many with the singing in them. You could hear the beautiful, rich Bahamian accent, almost like a different language. But there was a bonus with this boxlike electronic wonder, and that was Radio City.

As I would peer in thru the vent holes of the big radio, my imagination would come alive. With the insides all lit up from the glow of the tubes, the circuit boards and parts were like a little city, with its streets, intersections, houses, small buildings, round water towers, billboards, and skyscrapers. I would imagine myself down there on the street level, walking its streets, crossing intersections, and exploring that beautiful little electronic city. There seemed to be somewhere new to go each time.

Evidently there was a breakfast restaurant somewhere in there, as I eventually would come across the smell of breakfast wafting through the streets. I never did locate the restaurant. At about the time I would think I was getting close to it, something else would always seem to break my concentration. "Is everybody ready to eat? I've got a great breakfast this time," Dad would say, pulling me out of my little world and back into reality. His breakfast always smelled a lot like the restaurant's in Radio City.

Anyway, breakfast was a big deal for us. Once, back home, Dad decided to take us all out to breakfast. He took us up to the truck stop in Land O' Lakes, near our house. For some reason, he never took us back again. Maybe he thought we'd start to like it better than his cooking. Or something. Whatever the case was, the weekend cooking remained his. He loved cooking, and was good at it. Mom was our usual cook back home, but on the boat, Dad had his own recipes to experiment with. However, remember what I said about our provisions being limited. This meant that breakfast often involved seafood. Usually lobster. The creations were dishes like fish and eggs, lobster and bacon, lobster and corn bread, eggs and lobster, or lobster and eggs, depending on which there was more of.

Then, with breakfast over, it was time for us to do the dishes and Mom to get her dog rag busy cleaning up everything. Dog rag? What is that? —you ask. You'll have to wait until you read chapter six to find out!

CHAPTER FIVE:

Big Joe

C arter Cay is a tall, beautiful little island in the northern Bahama Islands and an intriguing place. But first let me tell you about how we came to know of it. We were anchored at a neighboring uninhabited island, about to spend the evening and night there after a long run in our boats from Grand Bahama Island. This was just part of our journey down to Marsh Harbor and Hope Town.

On this late afternoon, though, seemingly out of nowhere, a tiny boat with two men was spotted heading our way, and began to come alongside us. My dad was on high alert, as this was an unexpected visit in an area where we didn't think anybody lived. If they were just fellow seagoing travelers like us, where is their larger boat that they could travel with? Surely they were not exploring the out islands in a little dinghy. What did they want from us? Did their boat sink? We listened as they began to tell us who they were. It took us by complete surprise. We were all invited to a party! That's right, *a party!* They had a "secret" outpost on the next island over, Carter Cay. If this sounds a little fishy, be assured, this story gets even fishier. They explained that they were electronic technicians for a NASA rocket-tracking station, and the men worked for companies like RCA, Pan American, and others. It all sounded like they must be joking. They explained that there were more men back at Carter, about four in all. And that they had everything that should make up a home—electricity, running water, a fishing dock, a restaurant, and, of course, a full lounge with music, pool tables, Ping-Pong, dartboards, and other games. Everything you could want. Except for one thing. It was a very, very, lonely place. The men's families were not able to stay with them at their "paradise" home. It held too much in technology secrets. Besides, where would their kids go to school? The men had spotted our caravan of boats from their lookout place and had all decided to invite us over. Without us, of course, there would be no party. We were tempted to come and see if this was all true. As there were two other boats with us, they tempted our ladies and girls aboard with something completely irresistible: hot, freshwater showers. That's right, *fresh*, not salty seawater. It was all over. The four moms with us began to get giddy, with little laughs every now and then. One of them finally cracked, and we heard a "Why can't we just *go* and *see*?" In an instant it was unanimous among them. The dads caved, and agreed. We up-anchored, and all followed the little boat to Carter Cay, where we then docked.

It was exactly as the men had said. A castaway's dream. That night, at the party, there were the usual things you would have—food, games, music, dancing, and *stories*. However, one story in particular caught this eleven-year-old's attention. It was about a shark named

"Big Joe," a nickname given to him by the guys at Carter Cay and the locals who had crossed paths with him. Big Joe was "the biggest shark you would ever care to see," as the men put it. A few people had been able to hook him, but nothing could hold Big Joe. He would be seen on occasion navigating through the pass between the island and the next one over. There was no sense in even trying to catch him, they said. *That is, until now*, I thought to myself. I had heard all I needed to get the wheels of thought in my head turning. I exited the party with accomplice in tow—my little brother Joe. As we picked our way through the night, down the path to our boat, I laid out my plan. Our mission? To do what no one else could do—*Catch* Big Joe! My plan was really quite simple. Where others had used only rod-and-reel technology, I would "match the tackle to the fish," as Dad had taught me. *He'll be so proud*, I thought. I knew just the proper tackle. Yes, it was my time to shine, but also it was time for "The Hook," as it was affectionately called. Yes, the enormously big hook that my dad kept as a joke for use on his fishing buddies. The hook's hour to bask in the glory had also come. After all, it was for a time like this that "The Hook" was made.

The first step is to have a proper offering. Under the dock lights, I caught a nice mangrove snapper as bait. I actually contemplated keeping it to eat, as it was unusually large. *No*, I thought to myself, *Big Joe needs to be tempted with an appropriate dinner*. I took The Hook from Dad's tackle box. I knew also that nothing short of a clevis and three-eighths-inch dock line would do. I attached the rope to The Hook, and then the snapper. I then secured the rope to the main bow cleat, and tied it short, with no slack for Big Joe to run and cut it on the dock pilings. "There, the tackle matches the fish," I said, satisfied. After all, what fishing rod would be able to hold Big Joe? "This time, he's gonna bite off more than he can chew!" I said. Confident of our upcoming victory, my brother and I bedded down for the night, and eventually dozed off.

Then, *it happened. Bang!* went the shock through the boat. I don't even know exactly what time it was, before or after midnight, as there is really little reason to keep time out there, at least when you're a kid. But it happened all right, and I woke instantly, as if I knew it was coming. It seemed to be happening right on time, according to plan. The boat shook violently for a moment, the bow heaving downward, bobbing back up, and then bobbing a few somewhat lesser times until we sat calm again. *I have him!* I thought to myself. *Tomorrow, I'll haul his carcass on to the dock, amid the cheering crowds, and begin accepting their handshakes and congratulation, and maybe even gifts for a job well done.* This single act could propel me to the status of "The Best Fisherman." Tired but satisfied, I fell back to sleep.

When morning broke and it became light out, I scurried up to the front deck. It was, in a word, strange. All was quiet. The rope was still tied to the cleat. I expected that. But there was something wrong. The rope hung limp, slightly flopping in the gentle morning breeze. I quickly got down on my knees and looked over the side. Where was Big Joe? In fact, where was The Hook? I grabbed the rope and hauled the rig in. *What?* My bait, the snapper was gone. And, yes, the hook was still there, but it hung down pitifully, straightened, with just a slight curve now, where the bend in it used to be. "This can't be! This is terrible, I can't believe it!"

I had seen hooks get bent before, but nothing like this. I sat down on the deck, in shock and disappointment. It was all over. I'd had my chance, and lost miserably. I would not get another, as we would be leaving this little paradise-like corner of the world soon, to continue on our trek. As I thought about it, something began to occur to me. Some things I had not thought about before. Surely he was many years *older* than I. And this watery area was *his* world, *his* kingdom. Not mine. And me? Yes, what about me? Just another young, puny visitor to his kingdom. And he had kindly taken *my* offering!

Yes, I had been beaten, but I had been beaten by *the best*. The one and only Big Joe. That was at least some consolation. Everything considered, I felt honored to have crossed paths with him. I knew I'd never forget this one.

Consequently, as a side point, with Dad's help, I did have the chance to ponder the possibilities of that venture. I was helped to consider thoughts like: *What if the hook had held? That could have been really bad. What of the danger I had placed us in, with that large of a creature attached to our little boat?* There was no doubt. It was I who had ended up biting off more than I could chew.

. . .

OK, granted, the idea of catching Big Joe may not have been a great idea. But let's not focus on that. The real lesson is this: that we don't always get what we had hoped for, or planned for, but it doesn't stop us from trying our best. And a worthy, meaningful challenge really deserves our best. After all, who wants to look back after a failure and have to say with regrets: "If only I done more, if only I had done my best"? Catching Big Joe may not have really been an important thing, but in a way it was a step for me in giving something my very best effort.

So, especially when it comes to the important things, give it your best. You may not get straight A's in class. But that shouldn't stop you from trying to get there. That's all we can do. You'll walk away from things feeling good if it works out, or at least more satisfied with yourself if for some reason it doesn't work out.

Always take pride in what you do, no matter what the circumstances are.

. . .

The BOAT KID

CHAPTER SIX:

The Little Boat That Could

I figured a book like this has to have one of those stories about something that tried to beat the odds, by simply not giving up. So here it is.

It was as if the Atlantic Ocean was furious with the little boat for even attempting to enter its realm. Relentlessly, it tossed and slammed the little boat and its crew of five. Still, both wet and scared, they pressed on. It was like "The Little Train that Could" story, only in this case, it was a "little boat." That little boat was ours! And the people in it? You guessed it: my family. Amid it all, I asked myself: *How did we manage to get ourselves into this mess?* Let me explain.

It was a bad time to cross the Florida Straits as the windy weather was toying with us for the past couple of days. Our trio of boats was camping around Peanut Island, near Riviera Beach, which is near Palm Beach. We were hoping things would improve. They didn't. Everyone was getting the itch to just get going. The northern Bahama Islands were our destination, and the dads made a decision, to give it a try.

When morning broke, we headed out through the Lake Worth inlet, and faced the brutal Atlantic head-on, come what may. *It came.* Monstrous waves. Up we went, our bow rising high in the air, as if we were taking off in an airplane, only to level off, with the feeling of weightlessness. You then held your breath on the way back down, and then *Crash!* as we slammed back down flat into the water. Up again, weightlessness, and then again, *Crash!* The bow of our boat would sometimes submerge for a moment, then surface, sending the water on the bow up and over our windshield and gushing into the boat through the gaps between canvas snaps. This went on and on and on, repeatedly, every fifteen seconds or so.

Every jar, can, tool, piece of silverware, yes, it seemed as if everything with us sounded out its own high, loud percussion throughout the boat with each crash landing. We trudged over each giant, bone-crunching wave. The slamming and jarring would send the compass card spinning wildly out of control. Drawers would fly open, spilling out more of their contents, and then slam shut. There was nothing to say or do about it, as all of us were trying desperately to keep braced, and to anticipate exactly when the next crash landing would come. You had to have legs bent and stomach muscles set just right, at the right instant. You could not sit. No rear end is that hardy. Breakfast came back to greet us all, in the form of throw-up, and its unpleasant odor filled the boat. The jarring on our stomachs was just too much to bear. At this point, I began to think, *Can our little boat do this?*

I thought of how smart it was on Dad's was part to poly-foam our new twenty-four-foot Wellcraft boat. He, Mom, and I had gone down to the factory in Sarasota and ordered a new model of theirs. It was a Ray Hunt design, so we knew it had to be good for the open water. We had only taken it on one other trip so far, in the Keys. It was turning out to be a great boat, as it was somehow holding together. I wondered how the others behind us were faring—our friends in their John Allmand Seneca 23, and my aunt Rita and uncle Coyt in their twenty-four-foot Stamas. Dad had also helped them foam-fill the inner hulls of their boats to withstand this kind of anger from the ocean.

Then my mind drifted back to the peaceful, happy couple of days we had just spent at Peanut Island. With all the boats tied together off in the protected and calm, clear waters around this beautiful, Australian-pine tree covered island. I had snorkeled every square inch around the island each day, hunting fish, and exploring the rusting hulks of sunken barges. I too had finally felt that it was time to move on. Now I longed to be back, or doing anything but this agonizing crashing over the waves. Something a little calmer, maybe like being chased by a T-Rex. *Hmm. Maybe not.*

I then turned to noticing how our boats looked large earlier, but now they looked like toys, as I would watch them behind us, the entire bottoms of their hulls showing as the boats would launch sometimes almost fully out of the water as the huge wave would pass underneath them. *Would we decide to turn around? What if the hulls don't hold?* The question was, *could* we even turn around to pick them up if we had to? We could easily roll over in the ten-foot troughs. All these thoughts went through my head as we continued pounding along.

Then, it happened. No, we didn't become a submarine, and we didn't roll. It was only something that I saw. Something, way back, on the heaving and lowering horizon, well behind our group of boats. What was it? Even the boats with us would completely disappear from sight, and then reappear at the top of the wave, only to disappear again. *We are just little corks out here,* I thought. I kept my eyes focused on where I had seen it. *Did I really see anything at all? There it is again!* Now I knew there was something following us. I could only see the spray it made as it crashed down, as all of us were going far up on a crest, seeing all around, and then back down in the trough, with nothing in sight. Whatever it was would appear, and then it would be gone again. I focused each time on where I had seen it before. Trying to figure out *what* was making the spray. I must have watched it for an hour, almost forgetting our own critical situation. Noticing that ever so slowly, it was getting closer to us, *whatever it* was. After more time, it had caught up with the last boat in our caravan. It was fairly clear now: another boat, a small one. *Are they crazy?* The little boat tried desperately to stay up close behind the last boat in our group. Then, unexpectedly, I saw it begin to pass us, off to our starboard side. Now I knew they were crazy. *What kind of a super-boat is this?* As it came past our boat, I could see it was a small cabin-type runabout, with an outboard engine. *What are they trying to prove?* We watched in disbelief as the little boat pulled out ahead of us, jumping clear out of the water at times, its propeller throwing spray as it left and then reentered the water. It drew farther and farther ahead of us, until eventually it looked as it had when I first spotted it: just a faint hint of white spray as it would crash down into the next wave. They were clearly headed for the same destination as us: the westerly end of Grand Bahama Island. Finally, the little boat was completely gone from sight.

A few hours later, we made our entry into the marina at West End. All of us were badly beat-up from it all. We felt like we'd had the longest abdominal-and-legs workout ever. From having my jaw muscles clenched tight for so long, my teeth would not stop chattering for quite a while, which the adults thought was quite hilarious. Don't laugh! OK, I guess it was pretty funny.

We assessed the damage to everyone's boat. Stuff thrown everywhere in the cabins. Anything not bolted down was somewhere other than where we had put it. Water had forced its way into places it shouldn't be, ruining cardboard boxes and paper bags. But overall, we came out of it with little real damage. What we all needed was a day to just recover from it all.

Then, we remembered the little boat! Where was it? Did it sink, or did it make to where it was going? It should be here somewhere. We all thought the worst, and our designated emigrations requester (my dad) asked the dock master if anybody had made it across ahead of us.

Dad brought back the news. A little boat *had* come ashore shortly before us. It had *literally* come ashore, running up on to the beach on the north side of the Grand Bahama Hotel, near the pool. Later, we would find out why.

A young couple staying at the hotel came down to the marina and told us a harrowing story. They were from Winter Park, and were headed, like us, to the Bahamas for a real "vacation on the boat." They had been waiting to attempt the crossing of the open Atlantic waters also when they saw our boats leave to make the trip. They tried desperately to catch up with us and follow in our wake. But one wave was just too much for their little boat to take. On this terrible crash down onto the water, a huge hole was blown into the forward part of the hull, near the bow. They were taking on water fast, and did not know what to do. To turn around would be certain death, as we would know nothing of their plight. They made the decision to keep trying to catch up to us, and get ahead of us so that if they sank, we would come upon them.

The problem was this: there was a river of water coming in through the hole in the bow, and increasing. They were sinking, and it was only a matter of time. The water would enter the cabin, rush through the cockpit area, and then flow over the transom at the rear, or stern of the boat. This flow of water was carrying their belongings, food, and other things in the flow and out of the boat. The husband began to notice that the only way they would not sink was to go as fast as they could, staying out of the water as much as possible, and keep the water running out over the back as fast as it came in. We were dumbstruck as we listened. Rather than coming into the deep marina and sinking there on the spot, they decided to run the boat up on the beach at a high rate of speed, as any slowing down meant they would not reach the beach.

A couple of days later, with the boat's hole repaired by the locals, the couple motored their little boat into the marina. They docked next to our group to start their on-the-boat vacation, and finally got everything dried out that they still had. It was a twenty-foot Winner Baronet, a cabin-type, very nice-looking, with a ninety-horsepower Johnson outboard. It still looked so small, but not near as tiny as it did that day out on the rough ocean.

I thought about its brave husband-and-wife crew, and how their little boat had somehow carried them to safety. How that little thing did not come completely apart because of what it was put through is beyond anyone. I took a good, long look at it, admiringly.

I realized something. This was the real deal.

This was the *real* "little boat that could."

. . .

Never, ever give up.

. . .

The Dreaded Dog Rag!

Now the dog rag is a peculiar item. I really don't believe that many boats at all were equipped with this item. But ours was. And to us kids, it is one of the most feared things on the boat.

Interestingly, it doesn't start off that bad at all. Like a bullfrog or a flounder, its life starts as something different, and then changes over time. You see, at the beginning of the trip, it looks like an ordinary, harmless, new dish towel. The kind your mom would wash or dry dishes with. At this stage, you almost felt bad for it, because it was used for nearly everything. Washing dishes; wiping coffee spills, the table, and dirty faces; cleaning up fish guts, throw-up, corrosion, and anything else you could think of. It did it all.

There was only one problem with this: Mom would only bring one. You see, Mom loves the simple life. She always says that if she lived in an Indian teepee that would be just fine with her. So she loved life on the boat. It was simple. A little boat meant little to clean. A little boat only needs one dish towel, or so she reasoned. And so, little by little, the dish towel morphed, or changed into something, well, in a word, sinister. We would begin to notice a change in its color, growing ever darker. Diseased-looking stains would appear, and get worse. Oh sure, she'd wash it, but it wouldn't do much good. And then the holes would finally appear, giving it a face, a personality all its own, with a look that was downright scary. It had now fully gone to the dark side. It had become the next dreaded dog rag! It was the story of a good towel gone bad. The fully developed aroma from it was horrible, like matted, wet dog fur, thus earning its name to the fullest. And you would never know when it might be used to wipe *your* face next, which, if at the wrong time, could induce severe vomiting on the spot. We were sure that someday, they would be illegal.

At the end of the trip, with us kids unloading all the stuff from the boat, one of us would find it. With a stick, we would walk it to the garbage can, as if in a solemn funeral procession. Being careful to stay upwind from it, its limp, lifeless carcass would be dropped into the garbage can. "It can't hurt us anymore," Kathie would say. But deep in our minds, we all knew better. Next summer, a new dog rag would certainly rise up to take its place. But that would be next year. And a year's a long way off when you're a kid.

. . .

I must admit that even the dog rag made things fun and interesting, as you never knew who, where, and how it would strike next—your hands, or your face. And the great fun it was for us to see the other person get surprised by the smelly bite of the dreaded dog rag!

. . .

CHAPTER SEVEN:

The Best (Little) Fisherman

It was about the middle of the afternoon, on a nice calm day. Our boats would be docked for the rest of the day, and I was getting ready to do some fishing. Little did we know of the crazy chain of events that was about to unfold that otherwise lazy afternoon. My little brother, about seven years old and using his fishing rod, had just caught a small pinfish and still had him on the line. It was a serene scene indeed—all calm except for one thing, that is. Let me explain.

We had been staying a couple of days around the Grand Cays, diving and catching our meals for the day in the waters of Walkers Cay, Grand Cay, and Sale Cay. Our final destination would be Hope Town and Marsh Harbor, before turning back and making the return trip home. We had been given permission by the nice locals to use a remote dock that had been built on one of the deserted parts of the island. After a day out on the water, we would find our way back to the dock for some late-afternoon fun and then dinner on the dock. With all the boats tied to the dock, we could eat together, all of us, and maybe play cards by light of our gas lanterns.

The waters always were inhabited by a wide variety of creatures. Upon our returning, we would notice that an unusually large needlefish would greet us, staying off the dock a hundred feet or so. We found out later that this version of the needlefish was actually called the hound-fish, being about three feet long in size. Anyway, having a dock to use in the afternoons was always a treat, as we could get out of the boat and do what kids do best: work.   OK, we played. Having a dock, we would normally visit each other's boats very easily, get onto the small island, or maybe even do some more snorkeling (as if we hadn't done enough of that already that day!) You see, that is what we *would* have expected. But there was just one thing wrong with this place. No, make it *two* things wrong. Yes, two things that made this place scarier than old gas station's bathroom.

The first was that this particular dock was like no other we had been on before.

You see, this dock was a very long dock, but only a *partial* dock. That is, it had *some* of the walking boards that you stand on, but not all of them. It would have a couple of boards, then a couple of missing boards. This pattern of boards here, but no boards there went on and on for the whole length of the dock. Traversing it was like playing scary hopscotch. Only one false move or misstep, and you could fall through the gap and down into the water.

Mr. Cooper, one of the Grand Cay residents, explained that thieves had taken the boards. But it was not polite for people to take *everything* out there, so only *some* of the boards were taken. Now, for us kids, always playing, horsing around, and often distracted, this posed a real problem. You could accidentally disappear at any moment, falling through an empty space between boards. Not to mention getting some bad scrapes and wood slivers in the process.

As if that wasn't enough, as I had mentioned, there was a second thing wrong with this place, giving us one more thing for us to deal with. It was this second thing that made this hazard extremely scary for us kids. You see, there is this type of large, carnivorous fish called the barracuda. Some just call it the 'cuda. We had already seen how aggressive they can be, shearing fish from people's spears. Once, while we traveled at a good rate of speed in our boats, a huge 'cuda zoomed through the air, trying to catch my sister, *on the boat!* He narrowly missed her, and continued his speedy run over the boat, and back into the water. So as kids, we had a healthy fear of these fish.

You can imagine how we felt when we discovered the dock's terrible secret. Living just under the dock was the biggest, toothiest, creepiest, hungriest-looking barracuda we had ever seen. He seemed to have an appetite for young people, as he would follow us kids wherever we went, lurking in the water just a couple of feet below us. He had a nasty habit of snapping his toothy jaws at us as he inspected us from below. Sure, we'd each been in life-threatening situations before. After all, our boat has a family of five sharing one bathroom. Things could get edgy, and quick. But this kind of danger just felt well, different. Like a ticking bomb that could go off, but when? Yes, his presence just sapped the fun out of whatever it was we were doing as the thought of him down there gave us chills.

Boys being boys, each of us thought that *we* were the best fisherman in the group. However none of us could show any evidence of this. And I say "boys," because there were girls with us. Be it wisdom or humility, none of them claimed to be the best at this. Don't get me wrong. Girls are often better at things. That's right, I said it. Take for instance one that I met in the first grade. While showing me the way to the office on what was my first day at that school, she asked if she could tie my shoestrings, only the right way. That hurt. And it didn't end there. I was a fast runner. She was faster, faster than any of the boys, in fact. But a good friendship grew anyway. What started on a shoestring turned into a strong rope. Yes, they can be just plain better at some things, and you might as well be OK with it. Who knows, you may be married some day and then you'll realize how important learning this point is.

Well, back to the story. The girls with our convoy just didn't care about this title of "Best Fisherman." But to the boys, this is an important one, serious stuff. And so, over the course of a couple of days, all of the boys, at every chance we would get, tried to catch the old barracuda and be the great fishing hero, getting rid of this fun-robbing monster below us.

We tried everything. Small crabs, and big crabs. Live fish, dead fish, and half-dead fish. Breaded fish, broiled fish, fried fish, baked. SPAM, bacon, ham, cake. Alright, maybe not cake. But I think you get the idea here. He turned his nose up at everything, barely even looking at it. *What is it with him? How could a fish be uncatchable?* Each one of us thought he was the best fishermen and we could not catch him. It seemed he only wanted one thing: us. He was waiting for one of us to fall through. It was frightening. Would there be no end to his reign of terror?

This leads us back to the particularly peaceful afternoon I mentioned at the outset of this story. My little brother, with his pinfish still hooked and on the line, decided to cast him back out into the water as far as he could and enjoy the fun of catching the little fish all over again. He could enjoy reeling in the prize just one more time. This is a popular thing to do for the very young fishermen. Of course, older kids would have nothing to do with this practice.

Anyway, he cast the hapless fish way out, and began reeling him back in.

Then *it happened*, and it all happened so fast. First, there was a huge ruckus where the little fish landed in the water. We both watched in shock as the big needlefish lurking out there snapped up the little pinfish in a bounding leap, sending him high into the air. Now my brother had *two* fish on the line! He fought hard as we excitedly yelled out, "Hey everybody, we've got him!" The fish began performing aerial stunts and skipping across the water at a high speed, as we watched. Suddenly, there was a loud scream from behind us! I turned to see what was going on, not even wanting to take my eyes off the fish battle in front of us. It was Steven, one of the other boys, and he'd fallen through a space in the dock, and was barely hanging on, about to fall all the way into the water. Other kids, including some parents, were hop-scotching their way to rescue him before he was grabbed by the 'cuda. I turned to see what was going on with the needlefish, but something speeding like a torpedo, going about thirty miles per hour, caught my attention. It was not heading for Steven, but actually headed away from the dock, and straight for Joe's fishes on the line. The needlefish jumped again, and in a flash, the huge speeding torpedo thing grabbed the needlefish in midair, clamping its huge jaws around it. It was the 'cuda!

It was sheer craziness, almost silly, like something straight out of a Dr. Seuss book!

One fish, two fish, at the same time,
But now there's three, three fish on the line!

The monster was doing back flips, and somersaults while shaking the needlefish in his mouth. He leapt high out of the water in a magnificent acrobatic display that I will never forget. It truly was an incredible sight!   Then, the line went limp. In maybe fifteen or twenty seconds, it was all over. The line had broken, and all three fish were gone. My brother was still reeling in the line in disbelief over what had just happened. "Did you see that? Did you see that?"—as if we had all slept through it!

Thinking about it all later, I wondered, would Steven have fallen through the dock even if little brother hadn't caught the barracuda? If my brother had not caught the little pinfish, then he would not have been casting him out to play with. If he hadn't cast him out, he wouldn't have caught the needlefish. If he hadn't caught the needlefish, he wouldn't have caught the barracuda. If he hadn't caught the barracuda, Steven might not have needed saving to begin with. Or was he going to fall through the dock anyway? Which was it? I thought about it till my head hurt. *Okay, let's not over-think this.* I let it go.

Some things that happen can easily be traced back to our or someone else's actions. But with others it may be hard to put your finger on why some things happen the way they do. Sometimes chains of events just can't be dissected for you to reach any solid conclusions. Timing and unforeseen circumstances may rule what happens. In this case, I guess it really doesn't matter.   The end result was that Steven was saved. And the old barracuda didn't go away.

But that crazy chain of events did add up to one thing we were all *quite sure of.* We now had a *new* "Best Fisherman" title-holder. Undisputed.

. . .

I'm sure you guessed this one: yes, keep your ego under control. Thinking you're the best at something doesn't make you the best. And always be ready to improve. Maybe I'm not quite as good at something as I think I am. They say the "largest room is the room for improvement."

Most people are always ready to say what a good job you did on something—maybe some art, your

*school work, or something else. It's the same thing
they like to hear about themselves—the good things.
And for the most part, there's really nothing wrong
with that; we can usually find something good in
someone else's work.*

*But maybe on occasion, why not ask someone with
experience—Mom, Dad, your teachers—this
question: "How did I really do on this or that?" or
"What could I do better on it?" or "How could I
have handled this situation better?" Then, when
they answer, don't get upset or take offense at it. Be
glad for their observation and help on the matter.
And some of it might be very hard to take, such as
their thoughts on some personality issues that
others wish we would improve on. Maybe it's how
we answer them, or our temper. Maybe we seem
selfish to them. Will we overreact when they bring
up these things, or will we simply listen calmly to
what they have to say?*

*Keep in mind, some people will not wait for you to
ask them. They will just say it: "It's good, but
here's what you need to do. . . . Here's what you
need to work on." Then, thank them, and think over
what they said. It really might be an eye-opener to
improvement.*

. . .

Fire on the Beach!

You're still reading this? Well, we must be somewhat alike, if this kind of book interests you. After all, there's not a lot of disaster, mystery, or even any sinister characters in these stories. OK, I guess we could put the barracuda in that category.

However this part, you will find, is not about people running for their lives from some out-of-control fire sweeping across the island. Nope. That might make a good book of fiction someday, though. Let's save that thought for another book. This is a book of true stories. So if you want to know what really happened on the beach, read on!

Well, it was a breezy but warm night on an island that I cannot remember the name of, somewhere in the Florida Keys. Our boats were parked just off the beach shore, and all of us, several families that is, had just enjoyed another dinner on the beach. Our parents were sitting around doing what parents do best while on vacation: enjoying themselves by rehashing the funny things that had gone on (or, more commonly, gone wrong) that day, and getting a few more good laughs out of whatever it was.

Kids, of course, seem to always take a more aggressive approach to relaxing. It had to include some kind of action! A good game usually would do the trick.

One particular night, however, would prove to be different. The kids had our own little fire going, as we often did, to light up our beach playground. Boredom set in after a while, and a new game was about to be invented. Fiddler crabs, a type of small crab that uses a seashell as its home, were rounded up and thrown into the fire. A winner's crab was one that made out of the fire alive. As the shells heated up, they would scramble to be free of it, only to be consumed by the fire. OK, forget what I said earlier—maybe this story is a bit sinister. Because that's what Kathie and I thought about the game. It was bad, and just plain wrong.

My sister stood up and voiced her anger. "This is a really bad game!" She then left the group, and I followed.

Thankfully, our stand on that kind of entertainment must have made them lose interest in it, and that game was never played again. We would go back to playing our usual stuff.

Here is just a sampling of some of the games:

Scary story time: A favorite of the older kids, this one would wreak havoc on us younger ones, who would be half scared out of our wits. No game pieces required. Best if accompanied with some sort of prank at the end to really get us screaming and running for our lives.

Ice-down-your-bathing-suit game: Pretty well self-explanatory, this one. Best results if there are a few un-suspecting ones.

Skip-a-dollar: Participants gather us as many sand dollars as possible. Divide them to each thrower. Sand dollar is skipped across the water. Thrower with the most total skips wins. It's an inexpensive way to play around with (and lose) money.

Sand races: Find the part of the beach with the thickest, loosest, hardest-to-run-in sand, and have your relay races there. It's the slowest you've ever run, and the falls and spills are much more fun.

Crab-grab: Game pieces are simple: one crabby crab. That is, one lively, well-clawed, unwilling crab that hates games. A blue crab or ghost crab works well for this. Crab is very carefully passed from one person to the next. A pinch, or a scream, and you were out. (The scream usually accompanied the pinch, of course.) Crab is released, unharmed, but still can't stand games, or people for that matter.

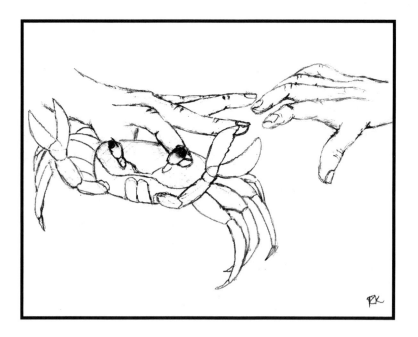

. . .

Life is full of choices, and it's no different when it comes to entertainment. Our choice of entertainment is one that we ourselves should make, so that we are sure it's a good choice. We don't need to join in with the group, just because it's what everybody else is doing. We don't have to "just go with it." When it's something that's just plain wrong, stay away from it.

Draw lines as to what you won't do, and stick with them. Listen to those signals when something tells you "this is not ok with me." And then act on it. It takes true courage to exercise justice, fairness, and impartiality. You may lose some friends along the way on this. But you might also change the way they feel about what they are doing.

. . .

The BOAT KID

CHAPTER EIGHT:

Lost in the Tar

The world can be a dangerous place when you are a kid. We all know of the dangers. Every kid does. You know, hazards such as being swallowed by a whale. Getting lost in a forest, or being pushed off a cliff by buffaloes. There's falling into holes that have no bottoms. Let's not forget quicksand, and even getting stuck in the grip of tar. Yes, getting thrown, lost somewhere, or stuck in something is what your nightmares are made of. Fear of being swallowed up and never getting out. Enough of that, and let's get on with the story.

It was another summer night on the boat, parked in the marina at West End, Grand Bahama Island. We had just enjoyed a dockside show at the marina where there was music, dancing, and performances, all by local Bahamians. There were tables of food spread out at the dock's edge for all of us boat people. It was a lot of fun. But for my sister, Kathie, and I, the night's festivities were far from over. Later, after the dinner, she and I went to the hotel's showing of a movie in the theater. It was one of those Greek mythology movies, this one with something about the son of the king finding "The Bell," and then going home to his father and reporting it.

After the movie, we began making our way out of the hotel and back to our boat. At some point, we must have made a wrong turn. Or two. OK, it may have been many, many wrong turns, but remember we *are* just kids.

"Lost" is a funny—as in *strange*—thing. Getting lost and admitting you're lost are almost two completely different things. Getting lost is often easy. Admitting you're lost is nearly impossible. This rule of thumb, for the most part, nearly always holds true, even as we get older. Dads are especially susceptible to succumbing to this rule. They will insist to the very end that they are not lost.

In fact, on that night after the movie, my sister and I passed in the outside covered walkway a family that was coming from their boat in the marina and was on their way to their hotel room. Following the "rule" to the letter, neither I nor my sister would just come out and use the word "lost" that night. We should have simply asked the family: *which way to the marina?* No, not us. Maybe, as kids, it comes from a concern for the other's mental well-being. You do not want to panic the other lost person with you. This may be some sort of unresearched mind-safety device to keep at least one person's head on straight while the other is melting inside out of shear fear. Whatever the case, it didn't work. We were really, really lost.

After trying different routes, and then exiting the buildings at one point, I saw a very welcome sign. I excitedly said, "Look! I see tall sailboat masts—that must be the marina!" Crazy-happy to have found our way, we ran down the walkways, past the pool area, and out to where we saw the masts. As we got close, there was something clearly wrong. We were at the *beach side.* The real marina, and our boat, was nowhere in sight. The boat masts were just the masts of the few excursion sailboats moored at the beach dock. Our situation had gone from bad to worse.

Depression began to set in. I cracked. "Why didn't we leave a trail of bread crumbs to find our way back? Then at least we wouldn't be *lost!*" I fired off to Kathie, in a pleading way. There. I had said it. I'd used "the word" *lost.* She looked at me, speechless for a while, like she was in shock. She was thinking. "Bread crumbs would only get eaten by the birds," came her answer. It was my turn to think. *Hmm.* She was right—birds. And lots of them, too. Let's see, there's: pelicans, cormorants, anhinga, and blue herons. Plus there's ducks, pigeons, seagulls and finches. Big ones outside, and little ones inside some parts of the corridors. (Yes, she was right, as she often was. My usual excuse for being wrong: She is after all, two years and five days older than me.) I stood and thought. *OK, not bread.* What about using peanuts, candy, popcorn, egg rolls, jelly beans, or just about anything! But there was just one problem. We take none of these items on our trips. But there was one thing. SPAM. Surely the birds would not be interested in that. It's only for humans. I could have neatly diced up some chunks before heading out to the movie. And the gel they pack it in at the factory would harden, and serve to cement the morsel in place where we had dropped it. It was perfect. I made a mental note for the next shore excursion. Actually, two mental notes, the second being to stow away an extra can of the stuff on each trip. While I had my stroke-of-genius moment, Kathie was trying to have hers.

"Why not get up as high as we can to look around to see if we can spot the marina," she said.

"OK," I replied. It was something. It was at least an idea. How could things get any worse, anyway? We found the elevator, got on, and headed to the top of the building. But of course, things could always get worse. And they did. We got a ways up, and the elevator just stopped dead. We felt like crying, but we didn't. OK, maybe a little teary-eyed. "I guess we should've taken the stairs," Kathie said. Then, as crazy as it sounds, the elevator decided to help us out, as it came back to life, and started heading up. Reaching the top, she said "follow me" and we ran to the end of the corridor, toward the window there. We both looked out, and all around. Nothing. No marina. We ran down the corridor in the other direction, found the window, *and it happened! There it was!* The marina below us in the distance, all lit up. And there was our Jersey boat! With the warm glow of the cabin lights, it never looked so good! We took note of how we would get from where we were to where we wanted to be. Yes, it was one of those great ideas that just sometimes just happens. Nothing could have been simpler. Looking down at the whole complex from up high, you could see that the place was really not as large as it seemed.

So, just where is the *"tar"* in this story? I'm sure you are wondering that. Well, if you must know, my sister and I had escaped from tar of a different kind. You see, we had been stuck in the grip of the *Jack Tar Hotel*, often referred to as "the Tar."

"So, how was the movie?" our parents asked when we finally stepped onto the boat.

"Good," we said. And I think that's about *all* we said, following the rule to the letter about not admitting being lost, and made our beds ready for the night. Brimming with confidence now, we made plans for tomorrow: Dad would send us on our run into the hotel for ice, and we would decide to play as elevator attendants for the guests. Another bad idea, but it was our plan. After all, as they say, "tomorrow is another day," with its own adventure and challenge. Oh yes, and don't forget the SPAM.

. . .

When difficult situations arise: stop,
think clearly, and look for the solution.
Stay calm, and don't panic.

We all need the help of others at times. But we have
to be open-minded enough to accept it, and humble
enough to even ask for it if need be. And there's no
place for pride when you're lost or need some kind
of help. Our own inexperience can cost us dearly if
we don't look to those who have experience, such as
our parents and trusted friends.

Others can help us see a situation from another
viewpoint we may not be seeing, as we may be so
close to the problem that we're just not seeing the
"big picture," so to speak. Often, we really need to
rise above it all to see what direction we need to go
in order to get where we want to be. So when you
need help with something, don't be too shy or too
prideful to ask.

. . .

CHAPTER NINE:

"SHALLOW!"

The day was beautiful and bright. We were under clear skies with only some small clouds here and there. It was about midday. There was not even a breeze, but it didn't matter, as we and two other families on their boats were making our own breeze by cruising at a good pace over a vast, open-water stretch of the Little Bahama Bank. It was the kind of day that was highly coveted by boat kids: almost perfectly calm waters, having that beautiful glassy look to them. No waves to toss you around. You could really enjoy the traveling to your destination, perhaps watching a lazy frigate bird high above you, cutting those wide, seemingly almost motionless circles, with no need to ever flap his wings. Or sometimes a pod of dolphins swimming toward our boats to visit for a while, staying just ahead of us and then disappearing. And you could see the white, sandy bottom of the world below you through the crystal clear water. It would seem as though we were not on a boat at all, but on some sort of airplane flying low over the desert below, with its wavy dunes and windswept ripples in the sand. It all seemed so surreal. Only an occasional fish or stingray scurrying away at our approach reminded us that there was actually *water* beneath us.

It was on days like this that Dad felt comfortable letting me take the helm. After giving me a compass heading for these long stretches of open water, he would then set out to do what he loved best. Which was: planning, fixing something that needed fixing, or, best of all, organizing The Box. This was, in his mind, a good time to organize, having all its contents scattered on the floor near the rear of the boat.

The unfortunate thing for me on this particular boat of ours was its type of compass. Yes, the vertical-card compass, but I'll explain that elsewhere in the book. Being a kid, I struggled with this type of compass, so Dad would often give me a cloud on the horizon to steer toward. Of course, clouds do change shape, and they have been known to move, and after some time, a new cloud would have to serve as my target. It was in this way that the other boats would follow our lead. From the air we must have looked like kites, all tethered together by our "ribbon" that was our wake. But, alas, the ribbon was not straight, but curvy, as whether I steered by compass or by moving cloud, I would lead our boats on a zigzag course. Even if it was ever so slight, it was a zigzag, and something that our fellow captains behind us would be sure to jokingly chastise us about later.

On days like this sometimes there was no horizon to speak of. The water and the sky seemed to become one and the same. We also knew that all this serenity could change very quickly out here, and become a mariner's nightmare. Yes, storms. On this one day things would change very quickly on me, but not in this way. You see, Christopher Columbus had named the spot we were at, five hundred years earlier. He named it La Gran Bajamar, (The Grand Bahamas) which means "The Great Shallows." That day I would find out just how appropriate that name is.

Then, yes, you guessed it. *It happened.* As I was sitting in the helmsman's chair steering my heading, my little brother approached me. "It's pretty shallow here," Joe said in a calm way. *What?* I thought as I spun my head to look out the side. He was right. Where there had been fifteen or so feet of water with a white, sandy bottom, we were now speeding over water that was only about two, maybe three feet deep, tops, and had a green sea grass bottom. *No, no, no,* I thought, *this can't be. What's wrong? I must be way off course. That's surely what it is. This is bad, really bad! What should I do?*

The day seemed totally different now. It seemed dark, and the beauty was gone. The fish, the dolphins, the birds—none of that mattered. I began to ponder. *Just why are we the ones who always have to lead? Why can't we be the ones to follow? My life would be so easy!*

I didn't dare look again. Stalling, I looked down at my brother instead. "Go look again," I said, and he headed to the back of the boat again, past our dad and all the scattered parts, so he could look over the side. After peering down and watching the shallow sea bottom still passing by underneath us, he finally made his way back to me, after passing Dad again, who was still working on his knees. "It's pretty bad," came his report. *Of course it's bad—what else would it possibly be?* I thought sarcastically. I mustered up the courage and took a look myself. Oh yes. He was right. Then came reflection time again. *How do these things happen to me? How did I get born into this family anyway? Maybe I can think my way out of this one. Yes, let's think about my options.*

Door number 1: Alert Dad. He will have me gently shut the throttles down, and set us into the mud and grass. We are stuck for hours on end, trudging our boats by hand through the muck. If this is already high tide, we may never get out. The verdict: I'm off course.

Door number 2: Don't do or say anything. Just keep going. The problem may go away, or we may run hard aground, with a lot of damage, and are stuck for hours. Or we may never get out. The verdict: I'm off course, of course.

Yes, it was the already-too-familiar "catch-22" situation, which is a situation in which you feel that you just can't win no matter what.

I did not have to think for long as to what I should do. *It happened* for me. "Shallow!"—came the yell from my dad at the back of the boat. "Shallow! Stop the boat! Stop the boat!" I pulled back slowly on the throttles, and as our boat slowed, we settled down into the grassy mud, stopping hard the last few feet. The other boats behind us did the same, and we all shut off our engines. I sat in the helmsman's chair and awaited my fate. We were going nowhere, but I wondered where all this was going to go for me. There was complete silence, but for me it was deafening. Everyone was scanning the horizon, looking for answers.

Dad began to take stock of the situation, and with the charts spread out, came up with his best idea and direction for us to go next. With the decision made, did we then start our engines? Oh, no. Instead, every person made their way over the side of their boats, easing our feet down deep into the mud. This not only freed up the boats as it lightened them, but gave everybody the job of pulling on ropes to inch the boats across the shallow, muddy grass flats. This is a very slow and arduous way to travel. With each step you take forward, your legs sink down into the mud, sometimes all the way to your knees. The kids would stay at the very front tip of the ropes, farthest away from the boat. That way, if we got stuck and couldn't pull our legs out, the boat would not run us over. As it turned out, we were not far from the end of the grass bank, and after pulling the boats along for about an hour or so, we were on our way again.

Dad had two things to say to me about it all. You can probably guess the first. Yes, I should have *said something*. The second, after his initial words of wisdom, was that I was not far off course. "It could have happened to anyone," he said consolingly. "Hey, at least you don't drive in circles!" We both laughed and enjoyed the moment. *I think I'll keep this family*, I thought to myself. However, I was certain that on the next time this happened, the others were going to just throw me overboard. As I'm sure they wanted to do that at other times. And yes, for some crazy, unknown reason we remained as the lead boat. Oh well.

"Hey Dad, can I drive the boat?"

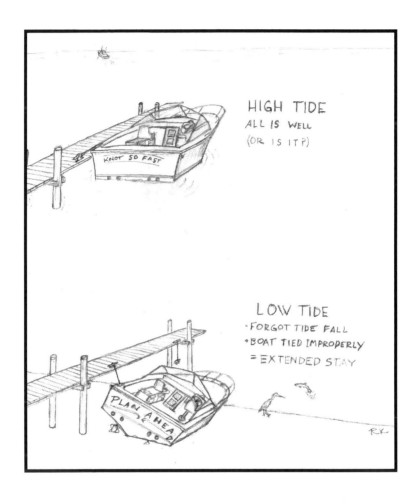

. . .

The question is, what would you have done? Which "door" would you have picked?

If you picked door number 1, you win!

That's right, sound the alert. I already knew that running hard aground can be really, really bad. Drives and props can get destroyed. There may be hull damage if there's a hard object like a coral head or oyster bar. Passengers, not braced and unsuspecting anything, go flying forward in the boat, crashing into things.

When you see a dangerous situation, or hazard that someone could get hurt on, you've got to do something, and fast. Closing your eyes to it is not the right thing to do. Keep everyone else's safety your business. This is not the time to worry about what others will say just because you were "off course."

It also helps to be forgiving after you correct someone less experienced. They will approach you with so many more of their problems if you are.

. . .

A Tale of Two Compasses:

Driving the boat was always fun, and kids like to be given responsibility. We feed on it. Helping to keep the boat on course is the compass, of course. But the compass does not steer the boat. Not on our boat, anyway. That would be our job. Read the compass, determine if you are off course, and get the boat back on track. Sounds pretty easy, right? Of course it is. But, as life is not simple, there is a flaw in the fun of navigation.

You see, there are two types of compasses commonly installed on a boat. The difference is in the way the card is built. By the way, the "card" is the dial on which the "north," "south," "east," and "west" are written. One type of compass, the card is flat, lying level with the horizon. But there is another type of compass, a mind-bending piece of work I call the vertical-card compass. The headings appear upright, in front of you. What was the difference between the two? Not much. Just that the horizontal one has the pointer at the back, and the vertical one has the pointer in the front. What does all this gibberish mean? Be patient, I'm getting to that. What it means is that with the vertical type, having the pointer in front, you have to think backward. When I would *think* it's telling me to steer to port (left), I'd have to remember to steer to starboard (right). It's just a characteristic because of the way this kind of compass is built. Now, mind you, this is not a problem for adults, but this is not any easy thing for this kid to do. I even had trouble with commands involving "your left," and "my left," for example. Why wasn't it *just* "left"? How can there be two lefts, with one being the *other* direction? Things like this bothered me to no end, and made me really wonder about adults. And don't bother watching the movie "Das Boot," (The Boat)—it won't help.

Yes, I had gotten spoiled for some time with the kid-friendly flat-card compass on our previous boat. It's what we kids trained on. The ones we got that came in the specially marked cereal boxes were all flat-card-type compasses. On the boat I describe in the "SHALLOW!" story, I had the misfortune of using a vertical-card compass, my dad's preference. That is why there was an awful lot of zigzagging going on when I was driving, as you will read about in that chapter. There, I've said it. Now you know: our notorious zigzag was not all my fault.

PART TWO:

At The Lake

For the fresh-water lover in you, the following stories are sodium-free, made only with fresh lake-water.

CHAPTER TEN

The Photograph

The young man looks unaware that his photo was about to be taken. While still in deep thought, he had turned to see who called his name. Caught completely off guard, the photo captured the moment, and his true feelings.

I now hold this photo in my hand. What is the story it tells? It is said that "one picture is better than a thousand words." We'll see about that.

I will try to tell the story in 999 words, or less.

I was coming around turn number three, and things were going great, I could just feel it. The boat was cornering with almost no hobble now. As it began to straighten out of the turn, I excitedly pushed the throttle all the way up to the stop. The powerful engine responded, and the boat leapt forward. A few seconds later came something that you could sense more than see, as even the slightest feeling of bumping or vibration from of the water's ripples disappeared. It is a feeling that is hard to describe, but this meant that the boat was now literally flying just inches above the water. My heart was pounding with the excitement. We were going to win with this one!

Was I dreaming? Was I really in a race? Well, sort of. Let me explain.

Dad loved racing boats, "hydroplanes" as this type is called. We had a couple of them, and several different engines that we would use, depending on whether we were racing in A, B, or D Class Stock Hydro. We also had our Switzercraft for racing the runabout class. We weren't big winners in it by any means, though. In fact, we never won. For the most part, the guys who were the winners spent big money on the latest, lightest boats, and bought or had built the best engine parts on the market. And then there's the devotion to the sport that you must have. Most of them no doubt took racing and winning very seriously. I, for one, wanted us to win. At least every once in a while it would be a nice change from just being in the race. But for Dad, it was just another family hobby. We visited towns like Lakeland, Frostproof, Tavares, Sebring, Mount Dora, and St. Petersburg. It was his therapy to be working on motors, and talking "boat tuning" with new people he met. There were the drivers' dinners, the friends, and the excitement of race day. It was all just great fun.

I have enough uncles to make your head spin. Let's see: Jim, Dave, Fred, Carl, Tom, Coyt, Cecil, and Warren. Each one of them is special in his own way.

Uncle Warren and my aunt, Judy, lived near us in Tampa. Young, tall, and good-looking, he seemed to have it all. They say an uncle is like your dad, only cooler. I guess your uncle seems that way because he's not the one who has to get after you about things when you need correction. That's your dad's job. Anyway, like my other uncles, he's really great and a lot of fun to be with. This meant we spent lots of time together. And he and my aunt would go to the boat races with us.

One night while we were at their house, over a card game, my uncle came out with it: "Ron, I need you to put together a hydro for me." My dad just looked at him, and then laughed. Surprised, my uncle responded: "What? What's so funny?"

"You can't race—you're just too big!" Dad was right. Most drivers were on the smaller side. My uncle was just a big guy. Every pound of weight made a difference on the boat and how well it would perform. My dad didn't even always pilot all his races. He had a driver named Ross, a sixteen-year old, to run our A Class Hydro and our Switzercraft. But my uncle was determined. "I really want to race, and I need you to help me with this." Dad was the kind who would always do so much for other people. You could guess the next part, and you'd be right. But I'll tell you the rest of this story anyway.

We located and bought a boat—a nice one, with a history of a few wins, but the owner was parting company with it. Next, we needed an engine. Dad began going through all his best engine blocks and came up with a Mark 55 Thunderbolt with cylinders and crankshaft still in pretty good shape. We located a Quicksilver or "quickie" midsection and lower unit. Streamlined, and with special gearing, they are what really makes the difference in speed. Many trips later to Interbay Marine for parts, and with lots of work until late in the night, Dad and I had the engine finished. I had learned how to replace reed valves, load a crank and pistons into a block, rebuild the carburetors, set a magneto's timing, and other things. Hanging the engine on the clothesline posts in our back yard; he let me spray-paint it, trusting me with this final, important touch. Checking on my work, I had runs in the paint that were more like mountain ranges. "It's OK—we'll just sand it off, and you can try it again," he said. Of course, I was to do the sanding! Many sheets of sandpaper, cans of paint, and blisters later, it looked great. I had learned the art of a professional-looking job, spray-can-painting style.

The boat got its share of a complete makeover too. Visiting T.A. Mahoney, Poston Marine Supply and Quality Coatings for the right supplies—and don't forget Harvey's Hardware, we got to work. We knew that until we changed the boat's looks entirely, it would always just be "the hydro that someone else owned." Picking out a nice metallic maroon color, we got going with Dad's compressor and paint sprayer. The results were dazzling.

Interestingly, my uncle saw none of this. Why would my dad do all this? I would ponder over this sometimes till late after going to bed. He was always so generous with his time.

Mounting the engine and rigging up the throttle and steering cables, we were finally ready for our first weekend of test runs. We had given the boat a complete makeover.

After a check to make sure all cylinders were firing, Dad had his start-up run out on the lake to check the engine for noises and smoothness. He came back in to the shore. Then something crazy happened. "You're going to run this one, until we get it right," he said to me. What? I thought to myself. This is a D Class Hydro, and I'm going to drive it? A little fearful but so excited that I could hardly stand it, all I could say was, "OK, really?" With the helmet and jacket on, I mounted up the beautiful steed. After a few quick instructions on its quirks, he cranked it up. I straightened the wheel and took off.

I had driven his Mark 25 and Hurricane-engine-equipped boats before. Unlike them, this one really blasted off, and I headed for the imaginary turn one on the lake. The high-strung four-cylinder engine seemed to just belt out the speed with every little uptick of the Quincy throttle. Cautious on that first run, and per Dad's instructions, I kept the engine at about half throttle to break it in. I made quite a few runs with it that day. On the next weekend, Dad said, "OK, it's time to see what it can do." I expected him to take over and drive it himself now. "Let's get some bricks and a car battery or two," he said. "Why?" I asked, still a bit confused.

"Well, what do you weigh?"

"About eighty-five pounds," I said.

"Your uncle Warren is more than two times that, we're going to have to duplicate his weight to know what we're doing." Securing the bricks and battery, I remembered the time I was running his B Class Hydro and, heading dead into the wind, I nearly had a blow-over as I flew past the Connor's dock. A blow-over is when the hydro's bow gets a little too airborne, and suddenly begins reaching for the sky, and ends up doing a complete back flip. Fortunately for me, it rose up at a sixty-degree angle or so, waddled on its tail for a few seconds, and then gently set back down. It all happened quickly, but I never forgot it. Incidentally, Mom had flipped Dad's Switzercraft in a turn on the lake a couple of years earlier, and I knew Dad was wanting to take precautions.

With the bricks secured, the boat handled differently now. It was now time for Dad to begin his tuning of the boat. As I would come around the turns, he would notice things, and would flag me in, asking my speed and changing things up. Over the next few weekends, we ran it and ran it, and then ran it some more, each time with me driving it. We tried different things like raising the engine higher on the transom, different propellers, carburetor settings, and turning fins. Our best running prop was then given to a fellow racer nicknamed "Pop" who was known as a master of propeller tweaking. It was as if the boat were a thoroughbred racehorse, learning how to run under the loving hands of the trainer. And amazing it was for me to see our speed go from mediocre to incredible. It just kept coming up—sixty-five, sixty-seven, sixty-nine. And then at seventy miles per hour, Dad knew we were in the hunt, with a boat that would qualify! Finally, we made that run that I told you about at the beginning of the story. We could win, I just knew it! Ending the run, I took off my helmet. "You're not going to believe it! It's just bumping past seventy-five miles per hour!" I excitedly said. It was the best we could do anyway, as we were out of time. We had to get my uncle introduced to his boat and have him get some quick practice runs in, as race weekend was coming up quickly.

I sometimes would lay awake at night and wonder about my dad. Why did he let me do all this?

Was it to keep me "in the game"—so to speak? It must be. I already knew what keeping someone else "in the game" was all about. When we played football or soccer with the other kids, you let the young ones touch the ball, hold the ball, you even let them throw the ball or kick it every now and then. Maybe not in every game, but at least sometimes they could feel like they're in the game, not just on the sideline spectators. The experience for them is priceless. I was sure this was what Dad was doing with me. He already knew I wanted to race boats too. But he was fearful for me. At one race, between heats, when everyone else was feverishly tweaking their boats for the next race, Dad didn't. Instead, he took me on a little tour through the pits to watch them. He pointed out things to me: "See those missing fingers on that guy? Ask him if he misses them." Farther down the pits, he pointed out another. "See those propeller chop marks across that guy's back? Got run over." And he showed me others. None were pretty. I got the point, but I was still determined. He told me that APBA rules said I had to be at least twelve years old. Whether that was accurate or not, I don't know, but Dad said when I turned thirteen, I could race.

At some point in time Dad told me that Uncle Warren had said that he had just ordered a new hydroplane, a Marchetti. I don't know why he did it, but he did. Maybe my uncle didn't think we could make it happen for him, I don't know. I was disappointed in him at first, for doing this, until later that night, when something changed. What changed was that the wheels in my head began to turn again, as they often did as I would lie awake at night and ponder things.

A plan took shape in my little head. It was a clear and simple plan, actually. Let me lay it out for you: A.) Uncle Warren races our boat at first. B.) Uncle Warren gets his new boat he ordered. C.) Our boat becomes *my* boat. And finally, D.) I would soon begin racing the boat. It was perfect, one of those flashes of genius that you hear of people having, but as of yet, I had not had my turn. It was so good that I even began to think that maybe it was also Dad's plan all along. Did he know early on that my uncle was going to buy a new boat? I didn't really care at that time. All that mattered was my plan. And the plan was coming together.

Next stop was race day. It was a day that seemed a long time in coming, though in reality the whole project from us buying the boat, to getting to race day was barely a couple of months. And now it was here. It happened so quickly that my uncle had not even received word back from the APBA on what his racing numbers would be for the boat. So Dad and I put the temporary "XX" markings on it. To do this, we used tape so that we could remove them after the race, and paint the assigned racing numbers on it when we got them.

It was a beautiful day on the shores of Lake Hollingsworth, in Lakeland, Florida. With songs like "Dizzy," "What Does It Take," "Tighter, Tighter," and "Sugar Sugar" blaring over the loudspeakers, we all began getting our hydroplanes set up for the day. Excitement was high with our race crew, which was just our families and a few friends. Many of the other teams came with their highly decorated and beautiful boats. We fired back, having my mom and my dad's sister, definitely giving us the prettiest race crew, in my opinion, anyway. But today we had our secret weapon: our new steed, both beautiful and fast. (Soon to become my boat, by the way.)

And there was the excitement over our new driver, my uncle. If he was nervous, it didn't show, as he exuded his usual confidence. Dad snapped a few pictures that morning.

The water was choppy that day, and a bit breezy. Many of the boats in the other classes were struggling, and there were some mishaps during qualifying runs. But we were in! Our big race was now moved to Sunday. We had done our part, and got us to this stage. The next step was up to my uncle, and it was simple: win.

The next day, conditions were still breezy and choppy. Then it came time for our race. One by one, they headed out to the course, and began forming the pack. There were so many boats! As they came around, and began approaching the grandstands, the starting gun went off. All throttles were opened, and instantly, the pack's sixty or so engine cylinders began to pound away at their limits. The scream from them all was almost deafening. The huge mass of rooster tails thrown high in the air from the semi-surfacing propellers was quite a sight to see. The race was on! From his position at about the center of the pack, uncle would have quite a ways to go for him to get to the number one position. In the first lap, he jumped ahead of several boats, and by a few laps later, he had caught up with the remaining lead boats! We were going crazy watching in the pits, as we just knew he could do it! All of our hard work was resting on this one team member now. It was all on him! We watched as my uncle's and two other boats flew across the water, drawn tight together, and approached the buoy in turn four. Each was vying for the inside of the turn, just to the right of the buoy. If he could just get the inside, he could probably grab the lead with our fast hydro. I could hardly bear to look. Could he do it?

Then, it happened. We could only watch in horror as spray and boat debris flew into the air. I said to myself: No, no, no, this is not happening! The "Ooh!" that came from the crowd finally sank into my head that told me this was real. My heart sank, and I thought I could just die right there on the spot. When the spray settled, we saw our boat, almost dead in the water, and appeared to be half-sunk. There was nothing we could do. The other two lead boats came past the grandstands, unscathed, and one of them took the flag to win.

With some of the rescue boats alongside him, our boat limped back to shore at a slow speed. It was gut-wrenching to see the damage. Much of the left side of the boat was completely torn off, and it was nearly full of water. Getting out of the boat, my uncle paused for a moment, and looked at us, on what was to have been our victory race. It is a mental photo, a snapshot in my head of a very distraught-faced uncle. I'm sure the look on all our faces was not what he wanted to see either.

First, I held back tears. Racers don't cry. OK, maybe I did cry a little. Then came the feelings of anger. *How could he do this to my boat?*

In the pits, he had a chance to explain what happened. But to me, at the time, it didn't matter. He said that as the three of them approached the buoy, he had to make a decision on whether he could squeeze in or not, to take the inside of the turn. He being the one joining the other two in an already tight spot, he made the last-second decision not to force his way in and cause a horrendously dangerous three-boat crash, and instead he would be forced to crash into the buoy on its left side, letting the other two boats have the "legal" right side of the buoy. It was the kind of thing that happens so fast that you really don't think it through, you just do it. Feelings, or something else just takes over. Later, other people get the unfair advantage of debating over whether or not it was the "smart" thing to do. In this case, of course, it was.

With our hydroplanes back home after the race, Dad took a good look at the boat. But it was no use. Like a thoroughbred racehorse with a broken leg, we knew its days were over. "You know, this thing's finished," he said. I didn't need to be convinced of that. We removed the Mark 55 engine and stripped the boat of most of the hardware. Then Dad set fire to it in a corner of the backyard, by the dock steps. It was a tough day, again, as I solemnly watched my (our) pride and joy go up in flames.

A couple of weekends later, we were up at my uncle and aunt's for dinner and card games. Uncle had gotten his new hydro, but first he wanted to show me something in the backyard. It was a go-cart he had picked up somewhere, and it needed an engine. Wow! I thought to myself. "Get in, and I'll push you around the yard!" he said. Eagerly, I did so, still not having said a word to him since we arrived at his house. A go-cart was just too much to resist.

As he pushed me around the yard, I made a circle, and heading back toward the walkway, something came into view. "Don't run over her flowers!" he yelled. I'm sure he expected me to turn at the last second, but I didn't. Yes, ran 'em right over. So there! Stopping, while puffing and panting, he said in a weary voice, "What did you do that for?" *Yes, why did I do that?* I thought quickly to myself. And just like that, I decided to put it all behind me. I didn't like these hurtful feelings inside. After all, the best things in life are not things. And the boat was just a thing. Uncles are not; they are people. Second, the boat never was really mine to begin with. It was my own selfish scheming that made me think it was. Why couldn't I be satisfied with just doing something for someone else? Why did I have to fall for the old *What's in it for me?* type of thinking? I'm sure he was really confused by how I was acting. "Don't worry, I'll fix it," I said to him about the flowers. And I did my best to put things back on track that night. Besides, he had a go-cart!

Dad put all of our racing stuff up for sale—the boats, equipment, parts, everything, until it was gone. Did he get his drive or motivation knocked out of him from the disastrous end of all our hard work? Or was it that I would be turning thirteen in only about a year now, and would remember what he said about me racing at thirteen? I don't know.

What I do know is that, as Forrest Gump once said, "and just like that," my racing days were over. Really, before they had even gotten started.

The invitations to race continued to be sent to us for long after that, as a reminder to all of us of those fun times.

Dad had snapped a few pictures that fateful morning of the race. But there's one photograph in particular that gives the story. It's the scene I describe at the front of this chapter. It would be much later, from this one "surprise" photo of my uncle next to the boat, that I would see his real apprehension over his first race. Something I was completely unaware of at the time. Similar to Ringo's song "Photograph"—"Now all I have is a photograph" to remind me of it all, and "the places we used to go."

But the story doesn't all end all that bad really. We still had one hydroplane boat left. Dad felt it was just too beat-up by then and wasn't worth enough for us to try to sell. It was our little blue, trusty A Class Hydro, my old favorite. He kept it for me, and it lived out its retirement days with me and our beloved King Lake. A photograph of us is also included in this book.

Lying awake at night, I thought. Did Dad really think nobody would want the little boat? Or was he instead thinking of me again? Hmm. I don't know. But I'd say the latter is the correct answer. Yes, that's it.

Don't bother with counting them. I just checked. That was about 3,600 words, so I didn't make it. Not even close. And it still doesn't tell me everything the picture says. But you're not me. So I'm going to include the photo for you to see. Then, you decide which is better: the picture, or the 3,600 words.

Maybe the answer is this: The picture *and* the story behind it.

. . .

You hold this photo in your hand,
It's meaning was unclear,
But means the world to those who know,
And now you also understand.

No, all of that wasn't a complete loss, by any means. We, or should I say "I," learned the value of teamwork, and what lots of effort can accomplish. You may not always win, but you still give it your best, and play your part. Take pride in what you do, no matter what the circumstances are.

It's not a bad thing to have high expectations of yourself and others, as long as you don't expect so much that you set yourself up for a fall when things don't work out as you thought they would. You have to recognize that life does not always go exactly as planned. There will be some failures along the way, some that can bring you to tears. There will be disappointments, whether because of your own actions, someone else's actions, or just other factors beyond our control. You may live with and be reminded of them for a long time.

But often, from something lost comes something gained, called "experience." Learn from it, adjust your thinking for next time, put it behind you, and move on!

. . .

The BOAT KID

CHAPTER ELEVEN:

First Boat

As I spun around, treading in the deep water, I finally caught sight of the boat. It appeared to be filling with water, already half-sunk. As I swam frantically towards it, the stern began to rise slightly, and little by little, the boat slipped beneath the waves. I was too late. I watched in horror, as the boat began its unseen descent to the bottom, never to be seen again.

Pretty traumatic, huh? Well, it was. But I might have failed to mention that this wasn't a real boat. Just a toy. Sorry, I guess that was an important detail.

Yes, everybody has had that special toy in their life. I'm sure you do too; you just haven't admitted it yet. You know the one you had a hard time letting go of. But you did. You may not have even wanted to let it go. Yes, for me it was a boat. How would you ever have guessed that? But not just any boat, this was a real, factory-made fiberglass boat. All of four feet long.

You see, there was a boat factory in Tampa, called Caprice Boats. Dad knew the owners and everybody else there. Some of my Saturday mornings were spent there as Dad talked (and bickered) with them over the best designs, materials, and boat building methods. Dad loved it, and I think both sides learned a lot. I would spend most of my time there watching and helping the workers in the plant. Once, they even let me use their new toy, the "chopper gun." No, it wasn't something you mount to a motorcycle. It was like a large paint sprayer, only it could shoot out the fiberglass mat chunks along with the resin. It may sound boring to you, but it really was impressive, and a lot of fun. While there, we would also pick up our supply of fiberglass, resin, and MEK for our latest boat projects.

One day while we were there, the guys in the plant called me over. They had a surprise for me. They had made for me a real, fiberglass boat. It just wasn't very big. Built the exact same way they build the real ones. It was fire-engine red, with a shiny gel coat finish, just like a real boat. Complete with v-hull, and a compound chine, or spray rail. I couldn't believe that they'd done this for me. Sure, there was no top, or deck to it. I guess they figured it was good enough as-is. And it was. I now had a real, fiberglass boat built by a *real* boat company! Not our garage. Suddenly, all those wooden ones I'd made were just toys.

I guarded the boat with my life. All the Mounds Bars in the world would not get me to take it down to the lake to play with it. But the kids would still try. It was tough, as I had to pass on a lot of Mounds Bars. The little boat was my trophy. But I eventually eased my grip on that thing and gave in to an idea that Dad and his skiing buddies came up with one day during one of Dad's ski-parties he would have: put a metal eye in the bow of the little boat, and attach a rope to it. Put a small person in the boat: me. Then pull it behind our ski boat at ludicrous-speed across the water. Send the little boat and hapless passenger slinging all over the place, slamming over huge waves, trying to hang on for dear life.

On weekends, after they'd tired themselves out from skiing, it was time for me to entertain them again. But I actually liked watching them all have fun laughing. Like a live rag-doll, I'd skid, spin, and roll across the water when they'd finally sling me out of the little boat. And I had learned something in the process. That your things are so much more fun when you share them with others, in this case, with adults!

One weekend, though, the little boat's bow had enough of it all. The resulting sinking is what you read of in the beginning of this story. Dad felt really bad about it, as he knew what it had meant to me. I never would have dreamed what would happen next.

Most of us can probably remember the first "real" thing that we ourselves actually owned. For some this may be a phone, a computer, or some other thing. It was special, because it seemed that everything before it was really just a toy. For me, yes, it was a boat. Not just any boat, mind you, but a real, homemade hydroplane-looking boat. . . . OK, maybe it still seems like it was a toy by some people's standards, but it was a real boat nonetheless. Hand-built by me and my father's loving, but often fiber-glassy hands. Fiberglass is very itchy stuff, by the way. In fact, I spent many nights lying awake, half-crazy from fiberglass itch, with school the next day. I'd even try to bite the stuff off my hands, which probably did at least give me a diet high in fiber, just not the good kind. Yes, itchiness, not just from this project, but from the many boat productions of my dad's over the years that I assisted in. However, this project was different for me: I was getting *a boat*! The hard part was waiting at home after school was over, from about three thirty p.m. to five p.m. for Dad to get home so we could get more done on it.

Then, one day, it was finally done. I had witnessed the birth of a real boat. Built by our own hands, my boat was finished, all nine feet of it. It was beautiful, sleek, and even just sitting still there in our garage, (aka "the boat factory") it just looked fast.

Next came the shopping for motors. I had heard people say that if you don't have any money, don't go shopping. And if you don't plan on spending anything, don't go shopping. But that's what happened. Dad had bought this very old, finicky, cantankerous motor—a nearly useless six- or seven-horsepower outboard motor—for free. The kind that would better used as a boat anchor than a boat motor. Did I mention *old*? The owner probably begged my dad to take it. No, change that—they probably *paid* him to take it—yes, that's it. But at the time, it didn't matter to me. It was a motor! And motors push boats! However, neither of us realized what we were in for.

After mounting it on the boat, we tinkered, worked, fiddled, played with, and wasted more time with that motor than either of us would have believed. It was a motor with a bad disposition. Sometimes, it ran, kind of. And when it did run, it didn't have enough power to pull the skin off a pudding. My dad finally saw only one solution, and he made his move. He came home with *another* one. Yes, another one. Identical to the first one, and with the same problems! I thought they had broken the mold when they'd made our motor, but evidently not. I was staring at its identical, evil twin.

"We'll put them both on the back of the boat so we can work on them at the same time," came my father's hopeful suggestion. *Why would my dad do all this?* I pondered. (For that answer, see "The Boats" at the end of the book) So work on them we did! Entire weekends spent working on those motors. *Maybe this is just too big of a project*, I began to think to myself. *Maybe we tried to tackle the impossible.*

And then, one day, *it happened.* I don't know what he did, or how, or which threatening words he muttered to the motors, but something crazy happened. They were *both* running! At the *same time!* My dad sensed that this was a rare moment. Yes, one of life's little victories, and I needed this one as my own. He shoved the throttles all the way over on both of the motors, and he then bailed out backward over the side of the boat, frogman style, as the boat began to gain speed.

In an instant, everything changed. Those are the kind of moments you wish the press was around for pictures, as a photo would have told the story by the look I had on my face. The expression on it would not be seen again any time soon. My boat might just as well have been the Miss

Budweiser hydroplane as I raced around the lake, at full speed, all of twenty miles per hour. The motors had given me my moment in time!

We tried a few more times that day to duplicate that magnificent run, but the motors just said no. I went in to tell Mom about my experience. Dad finally got one motor re-cranked, and he motored out on the lake and disappeared around the corner. After quite some time, he and the boat reappeared. I say "he and the boat," as he was *paddling* the boat. As he got closer, I could see why. Both motors were gone. Completely gone. He had motored into the deep lagoon around the corner in the lake, and had deposited the motors in their final resting (and rusting) place. A wave of a different kind of emotion swept over me. I was both in shock and relieved at the same time. Somehow, I understood what he did and that it needed to be this way. And I was OK with it. I also had this crazy thinking that the motors were finally getting what they wanted—a rest.

Not long after that, he brought home a good, reasonably new 9.8-horsepower outboard motor, which, as a ten-year-old, I was able to start quite easily by myself. I had the "real deal." as people say—yes, my first real boat. A usable boat to enjoy (and give rides to others). After all, what's a toy good for if you don't share the fun with others.

That wooden boat is surely long gone by now, but fiberglass lasts, so there is something that remains: There's a small, red, fiberglass boat sitting at the bottom of King Lake, about a hundred yards due south of the Pritchard's dock. Someday, I'm going to find it.

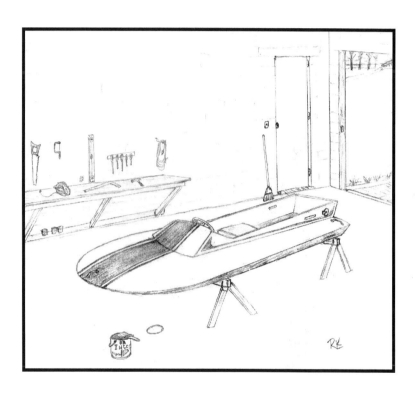

. . .

The first lesson is really quite simple, and may be repeatedly learned the hard way many times, or as often as necessary until we understand how true it is: you get what you pay for, pretty much. The rule applies to almost everything.

Often far harder to see—is that, like those motors, we may find many "free" or next-to-free, things in life that are really not free at all. They cost us in other ways—our time, our energy, and they may even wear us down mentally. Recognizing these, and the need to finally "cut bait" and make the change, is the hard part. And doing so before whatever it is really gets the best of us.

The third and most important thing is that in reality, it was my dad's hard work, and Moms' support and interest in the project that had given me that day. Many more like it will come because of their support.

By the way, Mom says a boat is still a toy no matter how big it is. I think she may be right.

. . .

CHAPTER TWELVE:

Ski Day!

L ying awake in my bed that night, I thought back on how this day was like no other. Really each day is kind of like a book page with nothing written in it, or so I have heard. *Today was just like that book page*, I thought, and considered how it all played out. I was in control of some things. Some of the things just happened. But all of it made for one great day.

It really started like any other Saturday morning. I got up at daybreak, before anyone else was awake, and quietly snuck through the house. Grabbing my Zebco 202 fishing rod in the garage, I ran out the back door, the same way I'd done a thousand times before. Another quick sprint through the lawn and down to the lake. Jumping completely over the steps and landing on the dock in one bounding leap. Now a quiet, slow sixty-five foot walk, and there I was at the end of the dock. Don't want to alert the fish. A short jump up the bench-seat back, and then my feet would finally come to rest on the top board of the handrail, next to the diving tower. Then, one final adjustment to the Bagley's Spring Tail worm. Eager for the first bass strike, I made my cast. That's generally how the first bit of every Saturday morning would go.

King Lake was my playground. Lots and lots of hours wasted there at the lake instead of being diligent at something, like watching TV. (Just kidding, of course. I was in a hurry like this nearly every Saturday morning because I had only about one short hour before *The Banana Splits Adventure Hour* would start.) There was fishing, as you just read, which taught me patience and to work at being good at something. Then there was working on perfecting the art of skim-boarding, on the sandy shallows at the lake's edge. I didn't need a computer, phone, or even fancy clothes. In fact, a pair of cutoff Levi's would work just fine. And then there was my all-time favorite, waterskiing. We had a little fourteen-foot-long ski boat that Dad and I had built in the garage, which we gave the name *Ski Thing*. With low sides, or "gunwales," and a wide beam, it was a fast little boat, fun to drive, and easy for us kids to get into. The problem was, with waterskiing, you need a boat and a *driver*. (And, for safety's sake, a spotter to keep an eye on the person skiing.) The launching and driving part fell on my good dad.

Making my weekend agenda, which always had "skiing" at the top of the list, was fairly easy for me. However, getting an adult's agenda to perfectly align with a ten-year-old's turns out to be more difficult.

On this particular summer day, about midmorning, I reminded Dad of my earlier request for him to take us skiing. This did not seem so difficult to me, as the lake was all of a hundred feet or so from our house. That's it. All he had to do was back the boat down to the water and take me skiing. What could be easier? The answer, of course, would be the all-too-often "no, I can't do it today."

However this one day would prove to be far different. I made my request to go skiing, and got a different kind of answer. "Well, do it *yourself*, then!" and he threw me the keys to his car.

Now, let me do some explaining here. Dad's car was a Ford Fairlane, with a V-8 engine, and a three-speed manual on-the-floor shifter we had installed, replacing the old steering column-mounted shifter that it had come with. So when he threw me the keys, we stared at each other for a long moment. Then I turned, and headed out the door, with keys still in hand. *He knows I can't do this*, I thought. *He's not expecting I will do anything at all.* Really, I did not imagine things would get very far. Then, I thought to myself, *I know where the gears are. And which pedal is which, and how to hook up the boat.* Still, I didn't know how this was going to work out.

I cranked the car anyway, and with a few stalls and re-cranks, the car edged its way over to the boat. Probably a half hour or so later, I finally had the car connected to the boat. Sitting on pillow-like cushions for height, incidentally, did not help as I then could not reach the car's pedals. I had to be content just to look *through* the steering wheel to decide which plants to run over.

With much backing and forwarding, weaving and stalling, the car and boat inched their way to the lake. A hundred feet was more like a hundred miles. Then there was the damage. *Nothing a pallet of sod can't fix*, I thought, as I looked at the trail of yard death I was leaving. I then began to notice that peculiar smell. It was a bad smell, and I had encountered it before. It was the same aroma that could be found at many a boat ramp, as a truck would slip, smoke, and burn its clutch out, struggling to get the boat up the ramp. Even the mightiest of trucks fell victim to "smoked clutch" syndrome. Undaunted, I pressed on, until success, at last! I had reached the water. I backed the rig down into the water with boat and car. *Not too far, as I don't want to get stuck*, I thought to myself.

Next step was to get the boat engine started. This was done by opening the front "door" of the engine cover, and grabbing hold of the pull-cord handle, like on your lawn mower. Now, your average lawn mower is about 3.5 horsepower. This boat's motor is *forty* horsepower. When you're ten years old, this is a nearly impossible task. Once you've got a good grip on the handle, you lean into the motor, and then push your body back away as hard as you can, like you're going to fall backward. All your weight begins to pull hard on that cord, and the motor begins to spin over, just barely. This process gets repeated quite a few times. *First, try choke* on. *Hmm. OK, try choke* off, until it finally sputtered and fired up, and I backed the boat off the trailer.

I was ecstatic. I had done it. I ran back to the house as it was time to give Dad the good news: that "skiing is on for today!"

"Well, so you really did it," he said, maybe trying not to act surprised. Thinking on it later, I was sure he watched the whole thing. Little did I know, the day's surprises were not over. My dad was an expert slalom skier—that is, using one ski as you go through the course. His personal favorite ski was his 1965 Dick Pope Competition slalom. I was OK on two skis, but always wanted to learn to ski on one ski, or "slalom ski" also, just like him. And so, that day, I gave it my best shot at learning this, or so I thought.

Thomas Edison would have been proud of me that day, as I invented every imaginable way you could possibly fall. I swerved, tumbled, spun, somersaulted, twirled, skidded, flipped, and flopped. Failing each time, I finally gave up. As I was floating there out in the lake after my last fall, Dad brought the boat up beside me. "I'm done with this," I said, as I pushed the nose of the ski up for him to grab it and put it in the boat. He didn't.

"You can't quit now; you didn't get it," he said in his teasing way he had.

"But I'm done trying," I whined.

"You can do it, you just haven't really tried."

What is he talking about? I thought. *I* have *been trying!*

"When you can do it, *then* you're done." He kept going right past me, not picking me up.

Is he getting even with me? I thought. Maybe he wasn't happy with me getting the boat down to the lake. I didn't know, but I didn't have a long time to think about it, as the rope handle was coming around, and I had better grab it and get ready to try again!

Once I had the handle, and both skis pointed up, with the rope straight between them, I gave the customary nod that I was ready. We surged forward, with my tired back and legs straining, but I was up. I did everything about the same way he had told me to do it before. I don't really know what or if I did anything any differently. Sliding my foot out of the boot, I let the left ski go. Then, dragging the left foot on the top of the water a short distance while getting that balancing thing down, I then eased my foot from the water, and slipped it into the ski's rear boot. *Then, it happened!* I was doing it! I'm sure I looked like a clown on a ski as I bobbed and weaved left and right, thinking I was falling with each, but then correcting it each time. So there I was, doing it! *Yes!* I made a quick look around to see who may be watching history being made (there wasn't anyone), and then, *SPLASH!*—down I went. *Why did I have to look around?* I thought, a little angry at myself. That moment was all of thirty seconds, but it didn't matter to me.

To the other kids on the lake or at school who didn't know me or couldn't remember or care to use my name, I was always just "the Boat Kid." But in my mind, I was now "Super-Skier." And actually, someone *was* watching—Dad. "Not bad at all," he said, which, when translated, means, "That was great! And I knew you could do it if you really tried!" Yes, I had done it, and from here on it would only get easier.

Later, Dad taught me his signature trick, the shore-start. With this start, you stand on one leg in just a few inches of water. Your other leg with the ski on it is held up about a foot over the water. The boat begins moving out on to the lake as you watch the rope be taken out. When there's only about ten feet of rope left, you signal to the boat, and the driver hits the throttle. When the rope goes tight about three seconds later, you jump up and forward with the leg you're standing on. This, plus the pull of the boat sends you flying forward, and you and your ski hit the water without you even getting wet!

Yes, it was quite a day. The page was complete, full, and well written. All because I didn't give up, or should I say, someone didn't let me give up on myself.

. . .

*A couple of things come to mind from that day.
First, be careful what you ask for. I'm not sure Dad
realized that I would really try to use his car.
(Though I would never recommend ten-year-olds
begin driving cars, this was at least in the confines
of our own backyard with no near neighbors or
other people around.)*

*Second, you may find others pushing you to learn
and accomplish things, whatever they may be. In my
case, Dad knew how badly I wanted it. (Not to drive
his car, but to ski.) If I would do all that with his
car, just to ski, why wouldn't I put forth that kind of
effort to learn slalom skiing? I needed that little
"push" to keep trying.*

*Like me, you may not recognize that caring push
that others may give you at times. Often, we even
resist, and may be even unthankful for their help at
the time. The appreciation for it will hopefully come
later. And then, thank them, if you didn't already.*

. . .

CHAPTER THIRTEEN:

Tippy Canoe

Winter is a tough time to endure for some water-lovers, like me. Because it usually means that not much boating is going on for us. Winter boat races we went to seemed few and far between. Sure, you could go down to the lake, which I would do, to catch the breeze coming off it. Sitting in the tree swing, I would try to imagine that the small ripples on the lake's surface were actually waves on the ocean. Boring, huh? Granted, but at least it beats watching stains on the living room carpet. Or in the evening as it darkened, there was taking the model wooden cabin cruiser boat I had made down to the lake. I'd put a lit candle in the cabin to give a realistic "night on the boat" look and set it out in the lake, complete with anchor and line.

One wintry day, walking home from the bus stop, Bill, who was walking with me said, "Hey, we could go out on my canoe!" *Hmm*, I thought. I began to ponder that. Then I began to savor the thought. *Yes. A canoe is still a boat, right?* Now, this kind of thinking went against all my better judgment. Setting my heart on a bad idea had gotten me in trouble before. And I had been on canoes before. They were great if you did not mind spending more time in the water than in the canoe, because that is inevitably the way things will go with canoes. The laws of physics are at work here. Using a canoe in the dead of winter seemed ludicrous to say the least. Cold water, hypothermia, runny noses equals lost school days and homework to catch up on.

"Let's do it!" I replied, throwing all logic and caution to the wind, and we put the plan into action. We each got home, changed our clothes, and a short while later Bill had paddled his canoe from his house to mine. I got in, we teetered for a moment, sat down, and headed out on the lake. All this, while knowing that yes, it was boating, but also knowing all too well it was just a bad idea.

Now, us being boys, the element of speed always enters the picture in nearly every activity we do. After some time, Bill said, "Lets see how fast we can get it going!" We paddled faster, and faster, and the canoe responded by giving us more and more speed. "You try coming a little farther to the back, and we can see if it goes faster," Bill said. I got off the front bench and sat a little further to the back. We were both still paddling as fast as we could, as the canoe plied along at a pretty good clip, its nose already off the water a little. "It's working, come further back!" he yelled.

Now let me explain a little about Bill. He was a scientific kind of kid, with calculations, and all that fancy sort of stuff. Science was his fun thing. Like the time I needed a report on volcanoes. So he had us build a miniature volcano on the lakeshore, complete with smoking moss inside and oozing mud for realism. It worked. Some of the kids even thought it was real. The photo got me extra credit.

But there is an important fact about Bill. He was a little bit older, a little bit smarter, and a whole lot *heavier* than me. We really didn't need to have me moving further to the back of the canoe. There was plenty of weight already there. It's kind of like stopping to buy fish tacos from a bait-shop. You just shouldn't do it. However, speed was calling, and speed we were going to get. In fact, we were going to get a whole lot more than we bargained for. Little did we know, but our old and consistent friend Mr. Physics was about to pay us a visit.

With the bow of the canoe already out of the water a little, and Bill's rear end nearly touching the water at the stern of the canoe, I jumped even farther back, now on the last support rung in the canoe, right in front of Bill. I picked up my paddling speed, all the while with Bill paddling as fast and hard as he could. We were sure this was setting a new canoe-speed record, for King Lake, at least.

Then, it happened. His last words were something like: "Wow, we're really flying!" But we had pushed things too far. The canoe gave a warning creak, then a groan, as it *raised its bow high* in defiance. It all happened so quickly, the bow heading skyward rapidly, until it felt as if it was straight up and down, like the *Titanic* just before its final dive. There was no time to think, or have him do fancy calculations on our angle.

If there had been witnesses to the event, they would have said they saw what looked like a monkey running at top speed, up the rungs of a ladder that was straight up and down over the water. That "monkey" was me of course, and that scared-out-of-his-wits monkey had reacted just in time. As I reached the very top, the canoe's bow began to fall, and then came crashing back down even faster than it had risen up. It slammed down into the water, throwing spray in every direction. We teetered, tottered, and then began to settle in, rocking gently. *Is Bill still there in the boat? Or did he tumble out the back?* flashed through my head. I knew that if he wasn't there, we could never get him back into the boat. We would eventually both end up in the water and be in big trouble. I spun around to look and see. A huge sigh of relief came over me as I saw Bill sitting there, still in his seat, each hand gripping a side of the canoe. His knuckles were white. His glasses were cocked sideways, and he had a dazed, shocked look on his face that I had never seen before, even after his wackiest experiments. His lower half was soaking wet. In fact, the canoe was about half-full of water. But the amazing thing was that *we were afloat*, with both of us *in* the boat, and that's all that mattered.

"Wahoo!" we both yelled, when our eyes met.

"That was some great climbing—I thought we were goners!" Bill said, grinning widely by now.

Even though there were no witnesses (that we knew of) to what had just happened, it didn't matter to us. We knew this was one we would not quickly forget. And, one that we would *not* care or dare to repeat!

Yes, there is actually a lesson from that potential disaster we had. Don't go against your better judgment on things. Even young kids like us are not impervious to the laws of physics. These laws are always there. They follow you everywhere, and you cannot get away from them. Because of this, they always have to be taken into consideration. Their evidence is there.

***Examples: 1.)** There's a reason why your bike has brakes.   **2.)** You can't put more weight into a boat than it can hold.   **3.)** Water becomes harder the faster your body hits it. (Trust me)   **4.)** Jumping off the roof is fun for about 1.2 seconds; four months in a body cast is not.   **5.)** You can't breathe water. (Trust me on this one, too)   **6.)** Looking directly into the sun is not the brightest thing you can do.*

But the point is that the laws of physics can be very unforgiving if you deny their existence, pushing things too far. Learn what you can about them. They are actually quite interesting. And instead of even attempting to push past their limits, learn to use them in your favor.

And don't confuse being courageous with being stupid or foolish. Courage is what is needed to exercise justice, or help someone in danger.   If someone dares you to do something dangerous or risky to "prove your courage," you can just walk away from it. Again, don't go against your better judgment on things. Always use good old common sense.

CHAPTER FOURTEEN:

Mudslinger's Monument

O *n the other side of the lake, there is a dock.*

There are, of course, many docks on the lake. This one extends out into the lake, like all the others. It's not that it is the longest of the docks. It's not that it is the shortest of the docks. It's even 'T' shaped like so many of the other docks. It's far across the lake from our dock, so at a distance, it looks like an ordinary dock. But there's something outstanding about this one, making it different from all the others. It's made of concrete. Solid concrete. Like a monument to stand the test of time. But this story is about what happened there, on the other side of the lake, in the clear, sandy shallows surrounding that dock.

Where do I begin with this one? It all happened so fast. There I was, on my skim-board, being pulled behind my teen-aged neighbor's boat. We were approaching the concrete dock where the yellow things were bobbing up and down in the water, splashing all around. As we went past them, *it happened.* I was plastered with mud balls that seemed to come out of nowhere. Big, mucky, yucky ones with nasty, smelly seaweed used to hold them together. My friend's little boat that was pulling me suffered the same fate. Battered from the mud balls, we retreated and headed back across the lake to the safety of our own shore and to lick our wounds.

The next week was almost a complete repeat. Blam! Smack! Splat! We were hit again. I seemed deaf for a moment, and thought the boat's motor had stopped. But it was just my ear taking a direct hit from a mud ball, almost knocking me senseless. The shaggy, yellow-haired bobbing things had done their dastardly deed, indeed.

Getting into the house, I headed for the bathroom. Washing my eyes out some more in the sink, Mom came to see what was going on with me.

"What happened? Did those bad people get you again?"

"Yep. And they're not people, Mom. I think they may just be kids," I added.

"Well, whatever or whoever they are, you're going to get knocked off your skim-board and get hurt." Still mystified, she added: "Why would they want to do this to you? And your shirt is ruined now. I should go over and talk to their mother," saying it in her always-calm way.

"Don't. I'll be okay" I said. "She sees the whole thing from her beach lounger. I think she enjoys it." As I walked away, she had one more thing to say.

"You know you don't *have* to go all the way over there anyway." She was right, but I let it go for now.

It was the "summer of love," or so we were told, but ironically there was not much of it happening on our lake.

Instead, it had turned it into an all out war zone. I had to come up with a plan.

Each morning when I got off the bus, I'd be looking. Passing by the kids on the walkways, and through the swirling masses in the hallways, I'd be looking, always looking, for just one of them, any of them, if I could recognize them at all. This would at least be a clue. *At least one of them, maybe more, goes to my school.* Then I could and should ask him some questions right then and there. "Who are you? How many are there of you guys? What are your names?" I could get to the bottom of it, like Mom would have wanted. But I didn't. I had suspects in mind, but I couldn't be sure.

So I made my plans. I had a lot of time to think it all out, too. There was always spare time in class. While the other kids had to think of what to draw for art period, I got started right away, as it was easy for me. Draw a boat. Sure, maybe not the same boat. I would change it up some. If it was a good one, I could usually sell it for a quarter to one of the other kids. But I was done in ten minutes or so. The rest of art time was mine.

Then there's the bus ride home. There was always lots of time for me to think on bus #15. My planning would be interrupted at times, though. Every day, after turning from Tower road, south on to Highway 41, our 1956 GMC bus would struggle to gain enough speed to make it up the overpass without stalling. Nearing the top, we'd now be at a slow, first-gear, agonizing crawl. The bus' struggle was concerning, and a hush would fall on everyone. This always broke my train of thought. Once over the hump, things would change to: trying to *stop*. The bus' brakes would holler and screech as it tried to slow down the runaway bus for the stop at Little Lake Thomas road for Michelle and her brother to get off.

And then there was the driver, Mr. Absher, who would pull the bus over, jump out of his seat, and sternly remind us that: "There's 66 seats on this bus, so sit down in one, now!" All would immediately comply.

But even amid all these distractions, and as the school year was ending, my plan still came together.

It was now the last day of school. While I sat waiting on the bus to leave and take us home, Denise tapped on my window. She rode 2nd bus home, so she always had lots of time to kill, and would visit me. "Can I see the watch?" was her request. This was an old, but working Timex watch my grandfather had given me. It was pretty much useless to me as I couldn't get the knack of reading the minute-hand yet. She loved the watch, but only liked me, or so she said. "Here, you take it for the summer," and I took it off and handed it down to her. She walked away, back towards the school, as she put the watch on.

I didn't imagine that over this summer there was going to be any problem at all. Nothing could go wrong, because: *I have a plan.*

I was wrong. The summer kept me busy with other things. Or should I say, Dad kept me doing so many projects that I didn't have time for what was important: the battle for the lake. I worked while I ate, to save time. I slept standing up. OK, it wasn't really that bad. But I was busy. We were building "Ski Thing" in our garage, a project that we would not complete until next year. While Dad was at work, I worked on whatever I was told to do on it. We also had to get my parent's eighteen-foot Seabreeze boat ready for their first trip to the Bahamas. We tested props, equipment, compass accuracy, fuel mileage, etc. And then we re-tested. Summer vacation was more like I had a full-time summer job, minus the paycheck. Little by little, my summer vacation slipped away.

While Dad and Mom were in the Bahamas, my brother, sister and I stayed at our grandparents' home in Tampa. Grandpa and Grandma took us on our first day back at school as our parents were still somewhere in the Bahamas.

With school back in gear now, it was time to get thinking again. The mud slingers across the lake were on my mind. I wanted to mount a complete surprise counter-attack as soon as possible. But my plan would have to change somewhat.

A few days later, I knocked on my neighbor Duane's door after he got home from school. This was the teenager with the boat at the beginning of this story. Duane was a lot older than me, but that didn't matter to either of us. He was already a junior at Chamberlain High School. He even had a '62 Falcon to drive to school, as it was in Hillsborough County, and we lived in Pasco County. They had moved next door to us the year before, and he wanted to finish school with the friends he grew up with. But more important than any of that is the fact that *he had a boat.* The one I mention at the outset of the story.

Now, there's something about boats I should have explained to you a long time ago. I just assume everyone thinks like me. It's a formula called *boat math.* Here's how it works:

Boats + People + Time = Possibilities. And Possibilities, if properly configured = Fun.

It's a great formula that's simple and easy to use. But after that, the math gets kind of skewed, as some Possibilities = *Trouble.* And we had found it in the mud slingers across the lake.

"So what's up?" Duane asked, when he came to the door. "Come on, you know! Let's take the boat out again and go get 'em!" I said.

He looked up and around, stalling. "I thought you had forgotten about all that."

"Why would I forget?" I replied. "I'm sure they're out there right now." "Maybe we just need to let it go for now," Duane said. "But I can't. We can't let them win. Look, I'll even carry the motor myself."

You see, if we wanted to use the boat, we had to carry the motor from his garage, down to the lake where his aluminum Jon boat was leaning up against the cypress trees.

Now the specifics on the little motor are as follows: Single cylinder, air-cooled, and with an integral fuel tank and two-blade propeller. It was branded at the factory as the "Clinton J-5," which Duane said stood for "Junky-5." Producing approximately four horsepower, (factory says five) though we swore we were squeezing around six out of it. It could have also doubled as a great boat anchor, weighing in at about forty pounds. This is why I was offering to carry it. To carry it was quite a feat in itself, for a guy who still had a couple of months before his ninth birthday.

"OK," lets go, I can study later" came his reply.

With Scott Mckenzie's "San Francisco" song in my head, we began our trek across the lake. Things were going great, I thought, as I trailed behind on my skim-board, loaded with my supply of mud balls.

I had my adjusted plan all set. This was really no more than a highly shortened version of my original plan.

As we neared, something was wrong. There was no splashing action in the water. No little yellow bobbing heads. In fact the whole place looked quite empty. The mom's beach lounger was gone. The mud slingers just weren't there. They were nowhere to be found.

We circled a few times, and headed home, very disappointed. Why? Well, not because I didn't get to slam them with mud. It was because I did not get to enact my plan. You see, my plan was to go like this: We would first unleash our fury on them, and then foolishly return. They were then going to slam me with mud, severely. I would fall, and then do the unexpected, causing a specially formulated chain of events to take place. *I would swim over to them with my board, and we'd finally meet.* We'd have a great time horsing around, and I would even show my new friends how to use a skim-board on their beach. It wasn't a good plan, it was a *great* plan. After all, they're just kids, like me. Who obviously love the water, like me. But the best made plans do not always go as planned.

In the days to follow I would gaze across the lake each day after school, scanning for the yellow bobbing, splashing things in the water. *Nothing at all.* Asking around, no one seemed to even know what happened with them.

The fact that I and others knew almost nothing about them only made it more of a mystery.

Yes, though the mud slingers were mysteriously gone, at least one thing did come back: My watch. Only for me to lose it later, permanently.

But there is one more little twist to this story. As you know by now, things are not always as they seem. Often, there is more to a story than you think.

You see, it was not them, but *I* who had lobbed that first, fateful mud ball one lazy afternoon. That's right. I was the culprit that had started this dirty little war of muck. You may have wondered: What was I doing *wearing* a shirt while skim boarding anyway? Well, I wasn't wearing it. I used it to hold the mud balls in place on my skim board. It's also why I didn't want Mom to get involved. And that would be why their mom seemed to enjoy my getting plastered with mud. Now you know the whole story.

So don't always presume that people have given you all the facts. Often there are two sides to a story. Before you judge it, get the facts from both sides.

Maybe someday, somehow, I'll get to meet those guys and we can laugh about it all. I might even let 'em toss a mud ball at me, for old-time's sake.

Sometimes there's a monument that is built to remember something that happened. And then sometimes it may have already been there. And a monument may not mean anything at all to anybody else who doesn't know the story.

Those mud slingers certainly won't be forgotten. Not by me, anyway.

Because:

On the other side of the lake, there is a dock.

. . .

Never put off things so long that it's too late to fix it. You never know when things can change, and you may not get the chance to say or do what you really needed to. Perhaps it's a long overdue apology. Or letting someone know how much you care. Fill in the blank here on what you need to do. Then do it or say it while it still can be done.

. . .

CONCLUSION:

Well, I do hope you have enjoyed these stories, but I have to cut this off somewhere. I could have written many more of them, as these cover only a few short years of the experiences that seem to carry more meaning than others.

You, of course, have or will have your own similar stories, for sure. It seems that the things most interesting to us can be what is seen through the eyes of someone young and experiencing so many things for the first time. The experiences can give us enjoyment to think back on, and may help get us through the more difficult times we all seem to face sooner or later.

Keep in mind that even though these vacations in the stories may sound as if they are all just fun and games that is *not* the case. It is more of an adventure. As some kind of travel is usually involved in an adventure, there comes a measure of risk that has to be weighed carefully. With that adventure comes also a lot of work. The participants, whether they're family or friends, must work as a team. All, including you, have to be patient, and be forgiving. You want to remember your experiences with pleasure, not heartache.

The truth is, your most memorable times don't need to come because you have a boat, or because you vacation at some exotic resort somewhere. Often, the best times we could enjoy and learn from can be cooked up at the local park, the beach, or even your own backyard. Add in family members, plus maybe a few friends, and stir well. Mix it up every once in a while by adding a baseball and bat, maybe a Frisbee, or skim-board (if you're at the beach), and you've got a great recipe for a ton of fun! Oh, and don't forget the olive sodas if you can get your hands on some! So put down that phone or handheld electronic gadget, get outside, and make some memories for yourself!

In closing, to any young person reading this, I would like to offer the following advice: Any experience you encounter, whether it's as large as a family vacation or as small as a smile from someone you know, is a gift to you, and nothing short of that. It is my sincere hope that your own experiences will be ones you can treasure for a lifetime.

The Boats: (If it interests you)

I could start off by mentioning Dad's first boat which he built when he was about ten, in Chicago. But he never got to use it as it was too big get out of the basement through the door. It's probably still down there, used as a coffee-table, a bench, or something.

So, needless to say, I also was smitten with this love of boats from an early age. My earliest memories of it all are of launching our boat near Lowry Park, then heading down the Hillsborough River. We would speed down river, past the always-choppy bend near the Tampa Armature Works docks. (This was because of all the work-boat activity that always seemed to be going on there). Along the way, much of the fun was waving to the police-boats and the men in the bridge-tender booths. They all knew Dad. Speeding along over the water, and heading out to the Sunshine Skyway Bridge, where we would catch kingfish, grouper. The return-trips were never remembered as I was in a state of unconscious exhaustion, which adults seem to call "napping." Entering school did not change things. While the other kids drew stick people and trees, I drew...you guessed it –boats. So you see, it seems only natural that my summer vacations are spent on a boat. Really now, where else would you want to spend your summer?

I will skip mention of all the many boats he had, but will stick to the ones that had an impact on us kids as they were the "vacation boats" so to speak.

The first being a 22-foot cabin cruiser type my dad built in the carport at our home in Tampa. It's the one I mention just above. Being constructed of plywood and fiberglass, and outfitted with twin Evinrude Starflite engines, it was extremely fast.

A little eighteen-foot Seabreeze boat started the Bahamas trips for Mom and Dad, a trip just the two of them alone made. They made landfall, but not exactly knowing where they were. But it was somewhere on the southern side of Grand Bahama Island, possibly close to Freeport. Seeing some people swimming and splashing in the water at a small settlement, they moved in close to ask some questions. They were immediately swamped with a dozen kids, soaking wet, climbing in, and jumping off, and then back in again. They didn't pay much attention to mom and dad, other than to stop momentarily to ask for candy, or cake. This went on for a time, as Dad and Mom tried to get one of them to settle down for a minute and at least tell them where they were. "We call it Diamond Head" came one answer, while all the mayhem of kids getting in, and jumping off the boat was going on. Dad politely tried to ask them to leave, but to no avail, as they were just too busy getting in and jumping off the boat. He then had an idea. He gathered up every quarter, dime and nickel he could find, and got everyone's attention, showing it to them in his hand. Then, while they all watched with eager eyes, he threw it out into the shallows, away from the boat. There was sheer madness as they all scrambled to dive for the prize. Immediately, Dad started the boat, and they eased away from the fun-lovers, leaving the fray behind.

Needless to say, next time they both would be a little better prepared. They would bring our larger Jersey boat, thirty feet long, and we kids would be coming along. (This is the trip I describe in the "Friends of Merritt" and "Lost in the Tar" stories.) Dad didn't want to motor the boat around the tip of Florida, so he and I built a trailer large enough to haul it over land, to West Palm Beach. This is what we did, and made their second trip to the Bahamas.

And they were not going to get lost again. Something called a "radio-direction finder," or RDF would make navigating at least a little easier. This was an electronic gadget that would pick up signals coming from different cities. The signals were beeps. Long beeps meant you would write down a dash (—). Short beeps you would write as a dot. (.) After listening to the signal, and writing them all out together, you would see a pattern. Then, you decide which city's signal it came from, with your book of city's signals. Then, mark the exact direction it came from on the map. Do this one more time with another city's signal. Draw its' line on the map. Where the two lines intersect, is where you were located out on the water! My job was to hold the compass still on the map, and keep the map pointed north while dad aimed the direction-finder for the strongest signal, which would appear on a small meter. (By the way the very compass and map we used to do most all of our navigating out there is shown on the front cover of the book.) The stronger the signal, the more exact the direction the signal was coming from.

This all sounds like a lot of fun, but I was often very seasick from it all, as we were out in deep open water, with no land in sight. A few throw-up spells from us kids would follow, and the making of Mom's dog-rag would be off to a good start from cleaning it all up.

Other trips were enjoyed on our next boat, smaller and easier to trailer. It was a 24 foot Wellcraft "Triumph-Vee," a deep-vee type hull as they are called, and it was designed by a boater named Ray Hunt. We took delivery on it three months after visiting the factory to verify their boat-building methods. We would come to find it had incredibly good characteristics. Many trips along the West coast of Florida, and the Keys, and Bahamas were had on this great boat. In time, we added a booth, cabinets, a deep-foamed ice chest, and other goodies, to make it as family-friendly as you can on 160 square feet of living space.

Special Thanks:

The islands themselves are not the Bahamas' only asset. The beauty of the friendliness and hospitality of their people, the Bahamians, made a deep impression on us. We'd walk into their settlements, to their stores and restaurants, barefoot, and they did not seem to mind us at all. They had welcoming smiles, and were always at ease to talk and laugh with us. I envied them, as their lives seemed simpler and more relaxed. It truly was a privilege to be able to visit them and enjoy their beautiful home.

The BOAT KID

Scrapbook of Photos

CHAPTERS FOUR and EIGHT: Mom, on our Jersey boat in the Marina at West End. The boat just to the right of ours belongs to the family we met there.

CHAPTER FIVE: At Carter Cay. The Channel in the distance is Big Joe's hunting grounds. Don't bother trying to catch him.

CHAPTER SIX: At West End's Marina. Cleaning up after a very rough time crossing the Straits. Our boat is farthest away, at the end.

CHAPTER SEVEN: Danger Dock, complete with missing boards and the menace lurking below.

Dad, cooking his specialty dinners.   Mom's happy because she's not having to cook.   Joe on right, with me behind him.   Hey, is that an olive soda?

CHAPTER   TEN

The Photograph

CHAPTER TEN
Dad, getting our boat ready for the race.

CHAPTER TEN
Me, with our little A-Class Hydro

ROBERT D. RAY
GOVERNOR

Office of the Governor

STATE CAPITOL
DES MOINES, IOWA 50319

July 20, 1972

Mr. Ronald R. Kinsella
Rt. 1 Boc 235-S
Land o'Lakes, Florida 33539

Dear Mr. Kinsella:

I hope you are planning to participate in the
A. P. B. A. National Stock Outboard Hydroplane
Championships in Cedar Rapids, August 21-27.
The Cedar Rapids Jaycees and the Hawkeye Stock
Outboard Club are going all out to make a truly
outstanding event.

Iowa's central location will help insure a record
turnout.

The many thousands of Iowa racing fans join with
me in inviting you to visit our state and the
many attractions it has to offer. Bring your
families and enjoy our Iowa hospitality.

Sincerely,

Robert D. Ray
Governor

RDR:cd

This would have been my chance to see Iowa,
but we had already quit racing by then.
Dad's middle initial is not "R", by the way.

CHAPTER TWELVE:
With one of Dad's creations: *"Ski Thing."*
Mom, me, and Joe.

CHAPTER THIRTEEN:
Cold winter breeze, at the lake.

CHAPTER TWO:
Kathy, with Happy.   (A.K.A. "Aquadog")

Me, in a wet-suit ad